BLACK AND RED

NEGRO AND NATIVE AMERICAN

Slave Owners in North America (1655-1865)

BLACK AND RED

NEGRO AND NATIVE AMERICAN

Slave Owners in North America (1655-1865)

COLONEL VAUGHAN WITTEN. PH.D.

CITI OF BOOKS

CITIOFBOOKS, INC.
3736 Eubank NE Suite A1
Albuquerque, NM 87111-3579
www.citiofbooks.com
Hotline: 1 (877) 389-2759
Fax: 1 (505) 930-7244

Ordering Information:

Quantity sales. Special discounts are available on quantity purchases by corporations, associations, and others. For details, contact the publisher at the address above.

Printed in the United States of America.

ISBN-13: Softcover 978-1-960952-95-0
eBook 978-1-960952-96-7
Hardback 978-1-963209-00-6

Library of Congress Control Number: 2023914693

TABLE OF CONTENTS

CHAPTER ONE

Origin and History of Slavery

The history of slavery spans many cultures, nationalities, and religions from ancient times to the present day. However, the social, economic, and legal positions of slaves were vastly different in different countries and systems of slavery in different times. Slavery can be traced back to the earliest records, such as the Mesopotamian Code of Hammurabi, circa 1620 BC, where it was considered an established institution, Archive from original Mesopotamia Code of Hammurabi, (2017).

Slavery is rare in hunter-gather populations because it was developed as a system of social stratification. Slavery was practiced in almost every ancient civilization, including ancient Egypt, ancient China, Assyria, Babylonia, Ancient Greece, India, the ancient Roman and Islamic Empires, Nubia and the pre-Columbian civilizations of the Americas. Their institutions were a mixture of debt slavery, punishment for crime, prisoners of war, child abandonment, and birth of slave children to slaves, Harris,W.V (1999) The treatment of slaves varied such as a famous Roman general in command of 80,000 men could be a slave to one powerful person who owned him for some reason and he would otherwise be free to do as he pleased, but had to obey his owner. North American slavery in the United States has been deemed by many as the most cruel form of slavery in that in addition to the control and punishment, it also separated the family, selling off wives and children to distant plantations and owners.

Although slavery is no longer legal today in any part of the world-it still EXISTS. According to the "Anti-Slavery Society" (2011), human trafficking remains an international problem and that it is estimated that 25-40 million people are enslaved today including about 60,000 in the United States. Mauritania is estimated to have 600,000 men, women and children enslaved as bonded laborers today, 20% of it population, "The Abolition season on BBC World Service" (December 2011).

Slavery in Africa

Slavery has existed in Africa for many centuries. Systems of servitude and slavery were common in many parts of the continent, as they were in most of the ancient world. In most African societies where slavery was prevalent, the enslaved people were not treated as chattel (property) slaves and were given certain rights in a system similar to indentured servitude elsewhere in the world. This was the case of the 20 captives/ indentured servants brought to the Jamestown, Virginia colony in 1619 and traded for food and water so the captured Dutch ship, commanded by a Spanish captain could continue on its journey, Ironbark Resources, Robert M Grooms, (2014), Ironbark Resources. The forms of slavery in Africa were primarily: Debt slavery, war captive slavery and criminal slavery.

Africa Forms of Slavery

The forms of slavery in Africa were closely related to kinship structures, "Inaugural Global Index... (2013)

Chattel Slavery: Is a specific servitude relationship where the slave is treated as the property of the owner. As such the owner is free to sell, trade, or treat the slave as he would other pieces of property and the children of the slaves are often retained as property of the master. This was the type of Slavery practiced in the United States.

Domestic Service Slavery: Often practiced in Africa, where slaves would work primarily in the house of the master but retain some freedom. Domestic slaves could be considered part of the master's household and would not be sold to others except for extreme causes. The slaves could own the profits from their labor, in land or products, and could marry and pass on their land to their children, "Anti-slavery Society (2011)

Pawnship Slavery: Was debt bondage slavery in Africa, which involved the use of people as collateral to secure the repayment of debt. Pawnship was the common form of slavery in West Africa prior to European contact, "Mauritanian MP, s pass slavery law", BBC News (2007).

Military Slavery: Involved the acquisition and training of conscripted military units which would retain the identity of military slaves after their service. These soldiers would serve heads of governments or an independent war lord who would send them out for money and his political interests," The Abolition Season-BBC" (2011). Slaves for Sacrifice: Human sacrifice was common in West Africa up to and including the 19th century. Slaves were the most common victims, Klein, Herbert S.; Ill, Ben Vinson, (2007).

CHAPTER TWO

Atlantic Slave Trade

The Atlantic slave trade or transatlantic slave trade took place across the Atlantic Ocean from the 15th to the 19th century.

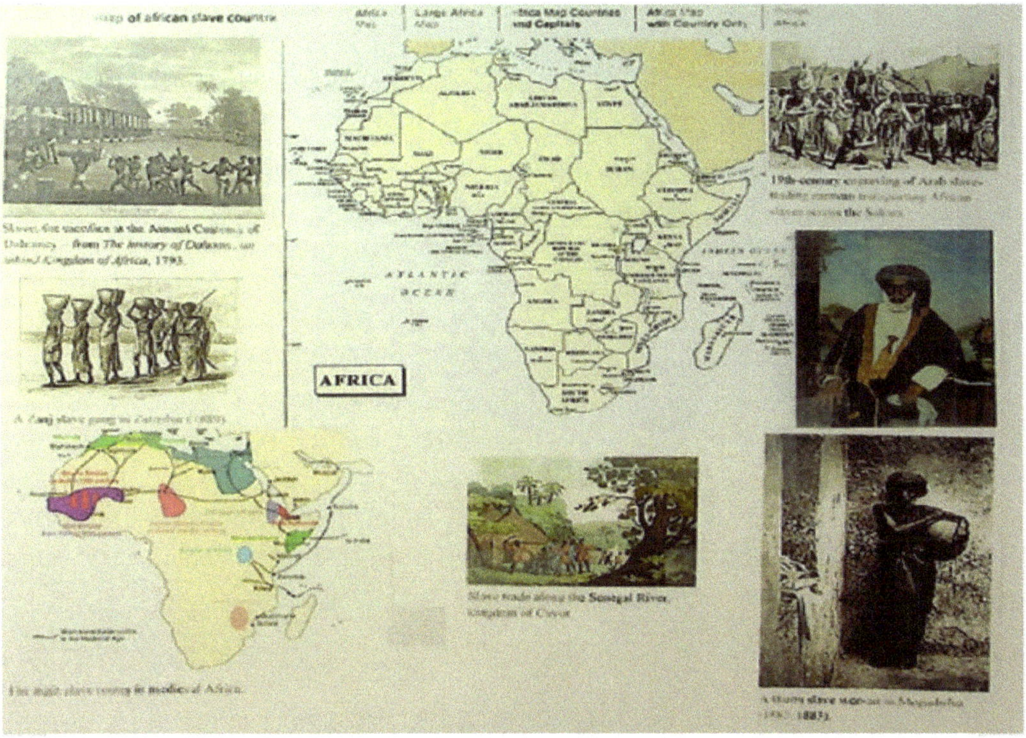

The Atlantic slave trade was significant in transforming Africans from a small percentage of the global population of slaves in 1600 into the overwhelming majority by 1800. The slave trade was transformed from a marginal aspect of the economies into the largest sector in a relatively short span, www.youtube.com.v=j50o2. In addition, agricultural plantations increased significantly and became a key aspect in many societies, Klein, H.S. (2007). It also changed the traditional distribution of the slave practices.

The first Europeans to arrive on the coast of Guinea were the Portuguese; the first European to actually buy enslaved Africans in the region of Guinea was Antao Goncalves, a Portuguese explorer in 1441, www.youtube/watch.v=N2mKW. Originally interested in trading mainly for gold and spices, they set up colonies on the uninhabited islands of San Tome. In the 16th century the Portuguese settlers found that these volcanic islands were ideal for growing sugar. Sugar growing is a labor-intensive undertaking and Portuguese settlers were difficult to attract due the heat, lack of infrastructure, and hard life. To cultivate the sugar the Portuguese turned to large numbers of enslaved Africans. Elmina Castle on the Gold Coast, originally built by African labor for the Portuguese in 1482 to control the gold trade, became an important depot for slaves that were to be transported to the New World.

The Spanish were the first Europeans to use enslaved Africans in the New World on island such as Cuba, Haiti and Dominican Republic (Hispaniola), www.bbc.com/news/world-africa, where the alarming death rate in the native population spurred the first royal laws protecting the native population in 1512-1513. The first enslaved Africans in Hispaniola in 1501 soon after the Papal Bull of 1493 gave almost all of the New World to Spain, www.theguardian.com/world/2017.

The Atlantic slave trade peaked in the late 18th century, when the largest number of slaves were captured on raiding expeditions into the interior of West Africa. The Increased demand for slaves due to the expansion of European colonial powers to the New World made the slave trade much more lucrative to the West African powers, leading to the establishment of a number of actual West African empires thriving on the slave trade, www.nation.co.ke/news/Africa. These included the Oyo/Yoruba, Kong Empire, Kingdom of Koya, Kingdom of Khasso, Ashanti Confederacy, and the Kingdom of Dahomey. These kingdoms relied on a militaristic culture of constant warfare to generate the great number of human captives required for trade with the Europeans, IBID. The gradual abolition of slavery in European colonial empires during the 19th century led to the decline and collapse of these empires. Emancipation would eventually follow and end legal slavery, www.bbc.com/Africa.

Abolition

Inconsistent emancipation efforts began in the mid-19th century. As European authorities began to take over large parts of inland Africa in the 1870s, the colonial policies on slavery were often confusing. For example, even when slavery was deemed illegal, colonial authorities would return escaped slaves to their masters, Klein, H.S., (2007). Slavery persisted in some countries under colonial rule and in some instances, it was not until independence that slavery practices were significantly transformed. Efforts by Europeans against slavery and the slave trade began in the late 18th century and had a large impact on slavery in Africa. Portugal was the first country on the continent to abolish slavery in metropolitan Portugal and Portuguese India in 1761, "Human sacrifice Britannica Encyclopedia, (2011), but this did not affect their colonies in Brazil and Portuguese Africa.

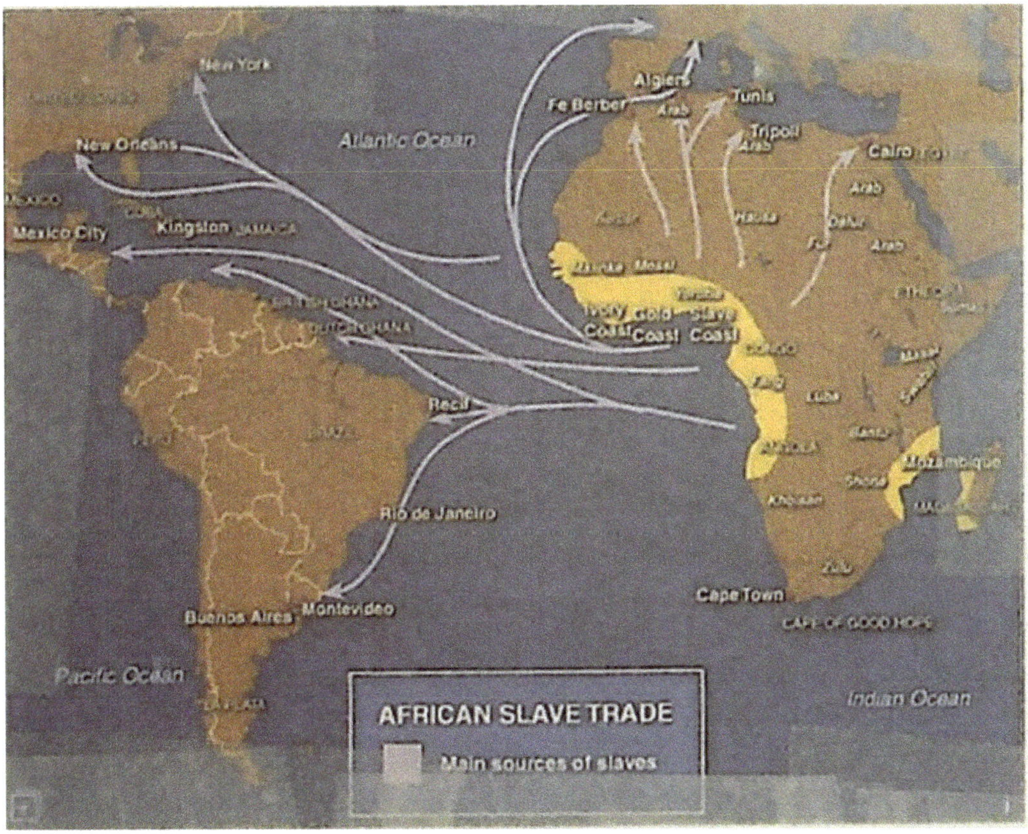

France abolished slavery in 1794. However, slavery was allowed by Napoleon inl802 and not abolished for good until 1848, IBID. Britain abolished slavery in 1833, and though the United States banned slave trade in 1820, slavery was not outlawed until 1865 as the result of a civil war that cost 600, 000 deaths in combat over this issue. Brazil finally abolished slavery in 1888. Slavery has never been completely eradicated in Africa and it commonly appears in African states, such as Chad, Ethiopia, Mali, and Sudan, in places where law and order has collapsed, "Warfare", www.Civilization.ca/haida/havwa. (2007)

Chapter Three

Slavery in the Americas

Before 1400: Slavery had existed in Europe from classical times and did not disappear with the collapse of the Roman Empire. Slavery remained common in Europe throughout the medieval period (dark ages). In 1441 the start of European slave trading in Africa began when Portuguese captain Antao Goncalves captured 12 Africans in Cabo Branco (modern Mauritania) and took them back to Portugal as slaves. In November 1493, Christopher Columbus on his second voyage to the New World, landing on and founding the first European colony: La Isabela on the island Hispaniola, (modern Dominican Republic), returning in 1496 with 30 Native American slaves.

In April 1500 Pedro Cabral of Portugal discovers Brazil and began bringing slaves to the new colony in 1502, to do the agricultural production of sugar and in the gold and silver mines, Maddison, A. (2008) When the Portuguese arrived in 1500, their situation as colonist was very different from that of Spain in Mexico and Peru. They did not find an advanced civilization with hoards of metals for plunder, or a social discipline and organization geared to provide steady tribute which they could appropriate. Brazilian natives were mainly hunter-gatherers, though some were moving towards agriculture using slash and burn techniques to cultivate manioc (cassava), a starchy root when processed is used to make bread and tapioca, (IBID). They had no towns, no domestic animals. They were stone age men and women, hunting game and fish, naked, illiterate innumerate, (IBID)

In the first century of settlement, it became clear that it was difficult to use Indians as slave labor. They were not docile, had high mortality when exposed to Western diseases, and could run away and hide easily. So, Portugal turned to imported African slaves for manual labor. They were pushed beyond the fringe of colonial society, their ultimate fate, similar to the fate of the American Indian. The main difference was greater miscegenation (sexual relations of men and women from a different race) with the white invaders and with black slaves in Brazil. Their most economically valued crop was sugar. Gold was discovered in the 1690s and Diamonds in the 1620s.

Gold production eventually collapsed and at the time of Brazilian independence in 1822, the main exports were sugar, cotton, and coffee. At the end of the colonial period half the population were slaves. They were worked to death after a few years of service and fed on a crude diet of beans and jerked beef. A few privileged whites were rich landowners, but most whites, mulattos, free blacks and Indians were poor. Slavery continued after independence, and finally abolished in 1888. It is estimated that 10 to 15 million African slaves were transported to the New World with 6% to North America and 35% to Brazil, (IBID). The population of Brazil today is approximately 208,000,000 people.

Map of African slave country:

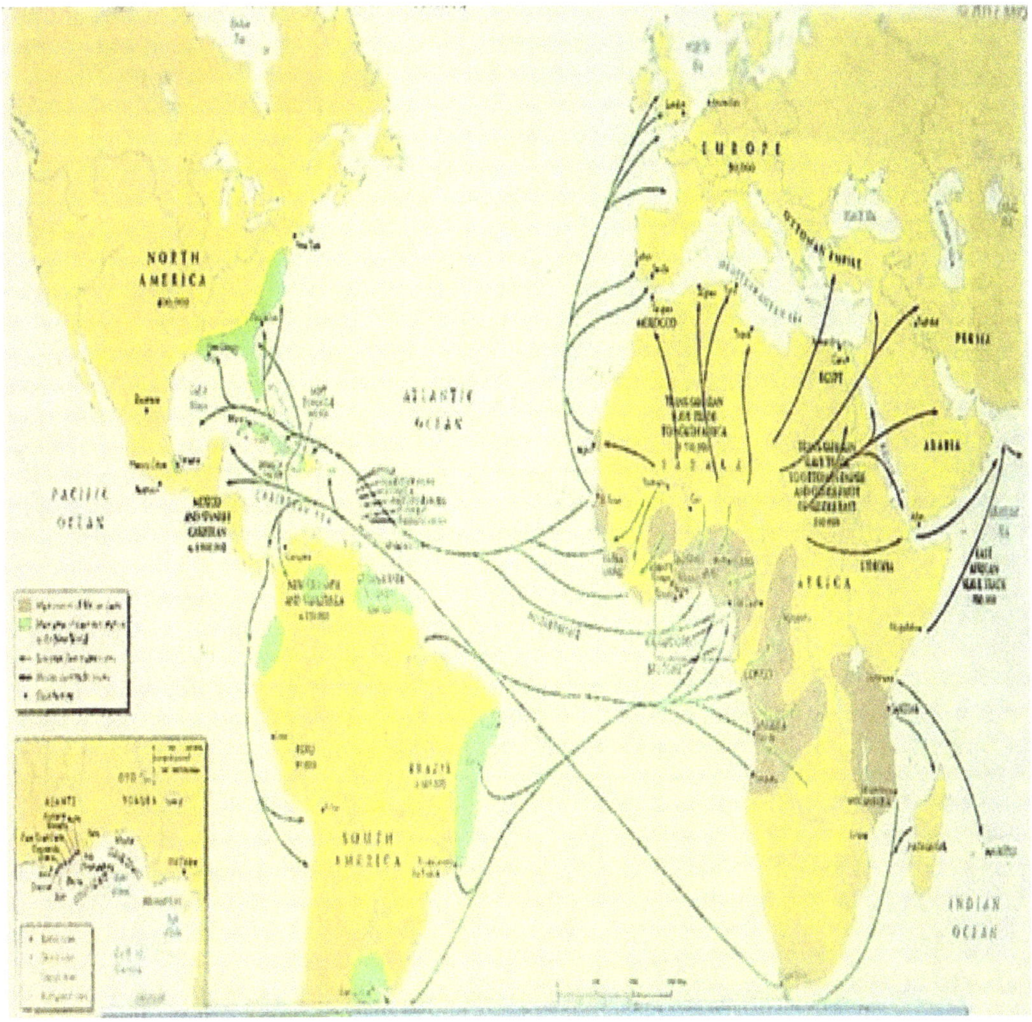

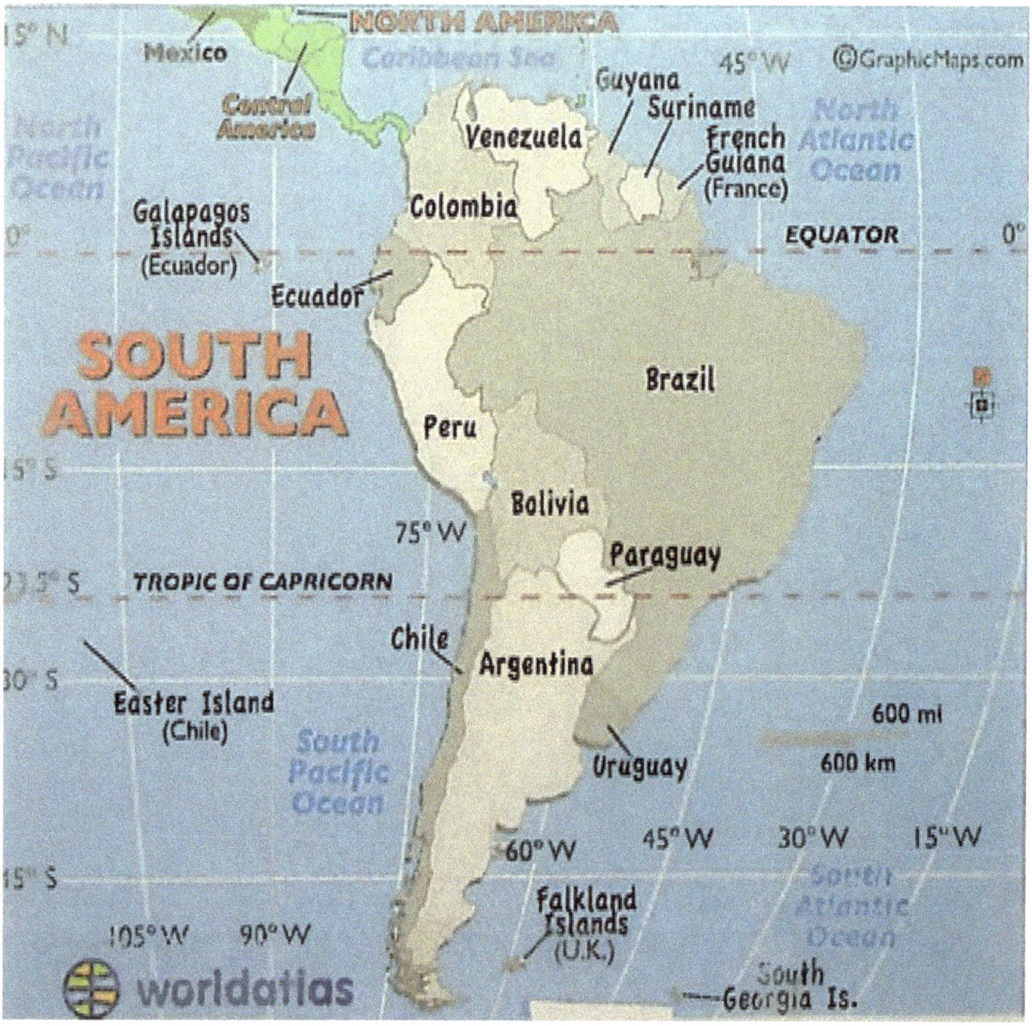

Slavery in the Spanish American colonies was an economic and social institution central to the operation of the Spanish Empire. Spanish enslavers justified their wealth and status earned at the expense of captive workers by portraying them as inferior beings and holding them as personal property (chattel slavery) often under barbarous conditions, Klein, H. & Vinson, B. (2007). In 1501 Spanish monarchs Ferdinand and Isabella granted permission of the colonist of the Caribbean to import African slaves. Proponents argued that the rapid decline of the Native American population required a consistent supply of reliable labor. In 1501 Spanish colonist began importing enslave Africans from the Iberian Peninsula to their Santo Domingo colony on the island of Hispaniola. These first Africans who had been enslaved in Europe before crossing the Atlantic, may have spoken Spanish and perhaps were even Christians, Gift, S. I. (2008). The Spanish enslavers used African slaves as workers to develop their agriculture and settlements. They also used them in defense of the colonies. The slave population was extremely low on Cuba and Puerto Rico until the 1760s, when the British took Havana, Cuba in 1762. Beginning in the 18th century, Spanish Florida attracted numerous

African slaves who escaped from British slavery in the Thirteen U.S. Colonies. Since 1623 the official Spanish policy was that any slave who reached Spanish soil and asked for refuge would be made a free man and given a lot of land to cultivate as a farmer. In exchange they were required to serve a number of years in the Spanish National Guard and convert to Catholicism, Riordan, P. (1996). The former slaves also found refuge among the Creek and Seminole Indian tribes, Native Americans who had established settlements in Florida at the invitation of the Spanish government. After the American Revolution, slaves from the State of Georgia and the Low Country escaped to Florida. The U.S. Army led increasingly frequent incursions into Spanish Florida, including the 1817-1818 campaign of Andrew Jackson that became known as First Seminole War. The United States effectively controlled East Florida. As Florida became a burden to Spain which could not afford to send settlers or garrisons, the Crown decided to cede the Florida territory to the United States in 1820, Deconde, A. (1963).

The Spanish American Wars of Independence emancipated most of the overseas territories of Spain; in Central and South America by 1853. The Spanish colonies in the Caribbean were among the last to abolish slavery. Spain abolished slavery in Puerto Rico in 1873, and in Cuba in 1886, from www.Wikipedia.free.encyclopedia, (2017).

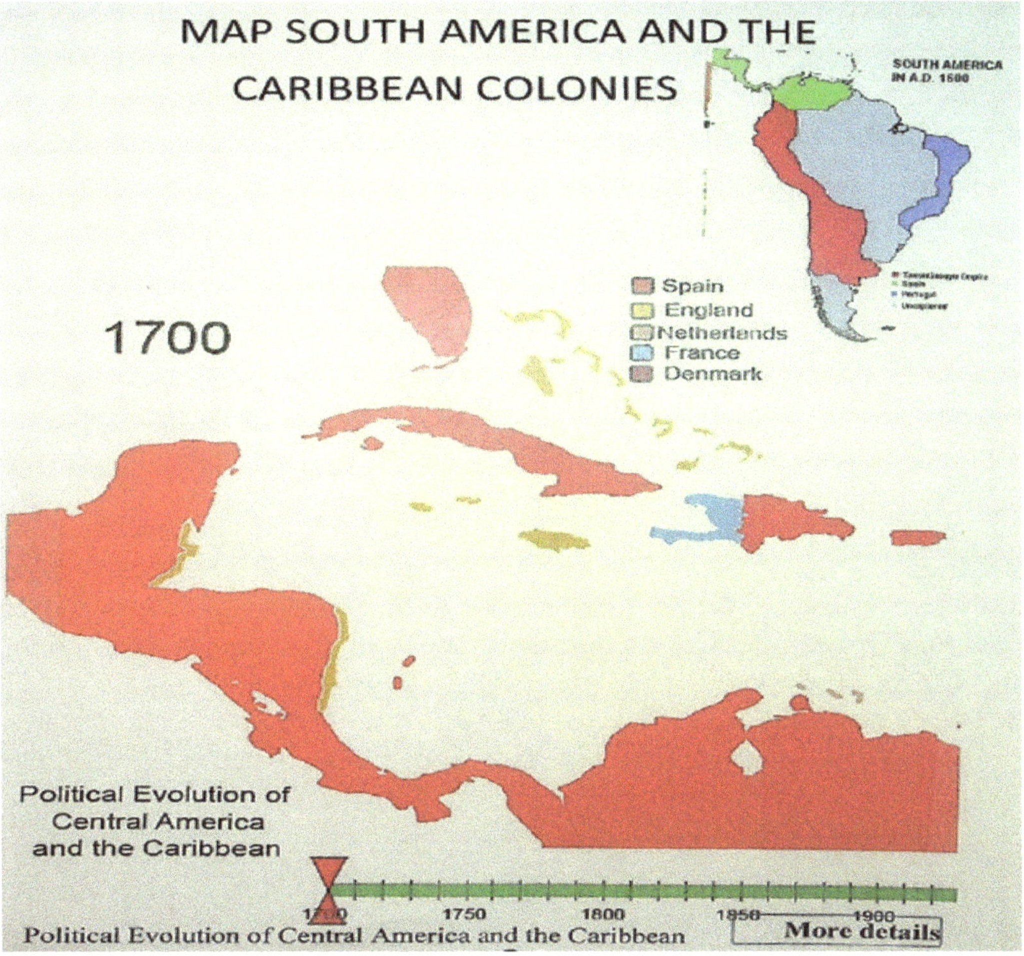

Chapter Four

Slavery in the United States and It's Justification

In the history of the United States of America, a Slave state was a U.S. state in which the practice of slavery was legal, and a Free state was one in which slavery was prohibited or being legally phased out. Historically, slavery had been practiced in all of the British colonies. The division between slave and free states began during the American Revolution (1775-1783). Slavery was a divisive issue and was the primary cause of the American Civil War.

The Thirteenth Amendment to the United States Constitution ratified in 1865 abolished slavery throughout the United States and the distinction ended, www.Wikipedia.free.encyclopedia, 2017.

Lifetime slavery in the U.S. did not start like a big instant bang. People were not brought here (Jamestown Va.) on purpose to be slaves in 1619. You might say it was accidental of a sort. How? You ask. Well, there was a Netherlands Dutch ship with 20 black captives (slaves), headed for some other place other than Virginia when it was raided and captured by a Spanish ship, which then needed repairs on the Dutch ship, along with food and water. They traded the captured Black Africans to the Virginia folks for the necessary provisions they desired. Then the Spanish captain sailed away to where? I'm not sure. But the people at Jamestown forced the 20 captives into 7 years of indentured service, a relatively short time, after which they were released, given land, a horse, seed and usually a pig to farm and make a life for themselves. This was NOT lifetime slavery, as it eventually became some 35 years later. And what is surprising is that the act that contributed to lifetime slavery was committed by a BLACK former indentured servant from servants. However, the Act of 1670 for bad Negros from owning Christian servants but conceded the right to own servants of their own race. By 1670, it was becoming customary to hold African servants as "slaves for life" and by 1681, what was customary became law, (IBID). And now for the Bomb Shell: Slavery as a perpetual institution is legalized based on a case before the Virginia House of Burgess by an African, who had been an indentured servant himself in Jamestown, Va. in 1621, and was known as Antonio the Negro according to the early records. He later Anglicized his name to Anthony Johnson. Anthony Johnson was believed to be the first Black to set foot on Virginia soil. He was the first Black indentured servant, the first free Black, and the first to establish a Black community, first Black landowner, first Black slave owner, and the first person, based on his court case to establish slavery legally in North America, (IBID). In 1635 Johnsons master, Nathaniel Littleton finally released him. As the custom was, he received a 250-acre plantation inl651 under the "head right system" by which the colonial government encouraged population growth by awarding 50 acres of land for every new servant brought to Virginia. He (Johnson) became the master of both black and white servants. In 1654 Anthony Johnson went to court and sued his white neighbor for keeping his Black servant John Castor who had ran away to the plantation of Robert Parker. Castor claimed that Johnson had kept him seven years longer than he should, so he (Castor) left the Johnson plantation. Johnson claimed to the court that he was entitled to Castor for his life. Johnson knew that if he lost the case that Castor could win damages from him, and he persisted to the court and claimed that Robert Parker had detained Castor "under the pretense that Castor was a free man". The court ruled in favor of Johnson saying that Castor was NOT free and had to be returned to Johnson for life. Parker had to pay court costs, (IBID). This case establishes perpetual servitude in North America; and it is ironic that the case was brought by an African who had arrived from Angola in 1621. Other slave owners then followed this ruling and began to hold their servants for life. Slavery was then basically established in 1654 when Anthony Johnson convinced the Virginia court that he was entitled to the lifetime service of John Castor. This was the first judicial approval of life servitude, except as punishment for a crime, (IBID). Further information regarding Black ownership of slaves will be revealed in another chapter, but for now we address the main topic of this chapter about slavery in general in the United States, and the religious justification the slave owners used to justify its practice. Slavery was legal and practiced in each of the Thirteen Colonies that became the United States. During British colonization the slave population expanded, primarily from the African slave trade, Wood, B. (2013). In the 1770s, blacks throughout New England began sending petitions to northern legislatures demanding freedom. By 1780 six northern states had abolished slavery, and by 1804, all of the northern states had abolished slavery or set measures in place to gradually reduce it, Painter, N.I. (2006). In the South, Kentucky was created a slave state from Virginia (1792), and Tennessee was created a slave state from North Carolina (1796). In 1808 the United States outlawed the international slave import trade, but the domestic trade in half the states continued. At the start of the Civil War there were 34 states in the Union of which 15 were slave states, Martis, K. C. (1994).

After the Civil War (1861-1865) slavery was abolished in all states in 1865.

Southern States' religious justification for the concept of slavery was based on Genesis 9:25-27. According to the Bible, the worldwide flood had concluded and there were only 8 humans alive on the earth: Noah, his wife, and their 6 sons and daughters in law. Noah's son Ham had seen " the nakedness of his father". Genesis

9:20-27 tells the story of Noah and Ham. After the flood, Noah became a farmer and planted a vineyard, eventually getting drunk from the wine produced. While drunk, he also became naked within his tent and was seen by Ham who told his brothers Shem and Japeth. The latter two backed into Noah's tent in order to cover him without being seen. When Noah awakened, he knew what Ham had done and pronounced the curse (Genesis 9: 27-29) which was to be the standard explanation for the origin of slavery. This particular proof of the divine sanction of slavery was quoted extensively in the proslavery literature, Richard Furman, (Exposition of the views of the Baptists Relative to the colored Population in the United States, 2nd ed (1823). Larry R Morrison, (2013).

So, Noah laid the curse—not on Ham but on Canaan, Noah's grandson. The sin had been transferred for some reason. So, what was the curse? Genesis 9:25-27: " Cursed be Canaan! The lowest of slaves will be to his brothers". He also said, "Blessed be the Lord, the God of Shem! May Canaan be the slave of Shem. May God extend the territory of Japeth; may Japeth live in the tents of Shem and may Canaan be his slave". Christian's tradition ally believed that Canaan had settled in Africa. The dark skin of Africans became associated with this "curse of Ham". Thus, slavery of Africans became religiously justifiable, Anthony Pagden-Human Slavery, (1998).

As far as the New Testament was concerned the major passage Southerners found which accepted, even justified, slavery was the Epistle (letter) of St Paul to Philemon, sometimes referred to as the Pauline Mandate. Onesimus was the slave to Philemon: he ran away from his master and fled to Rome where he was converted by St Paul. However, this conversion changed nothing; St Paul sent Onesimus back to Philemon, Dalcho, Fred Erick, (1823), a South Carolina Episcopal clergyman. Dalcho went so far as to claim that this Epistle really sanctioned.

The fugitive slave law because "slaves should not be taken or detained from their master without their master's consent", Dalcho, F. (1819) Practical Considerations. There were many other references to slavery in the Old Testament too numerous to mention. The Southerner's even referred to Abraham as having Hagar as a slave and procreated a child Ishmael, when Abraham's wife Saria was barren but later gave birth to Isaac. Finally, they argued from the reverse side that God has spoken through his prophets for over two thousand years and none of them has condemned or opposed the practice of holding slaves, therefore slavery had to be acceptable to God.

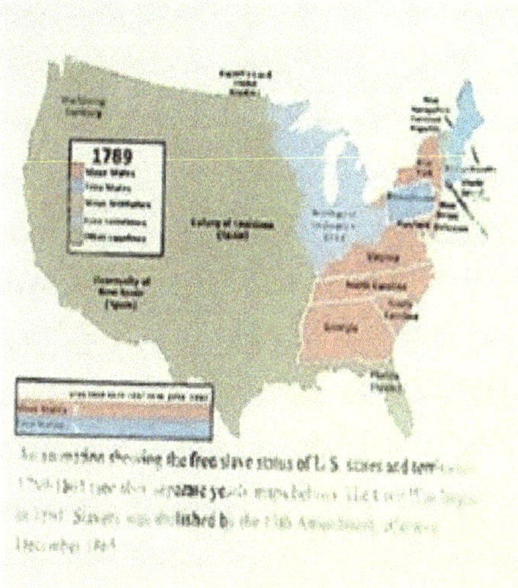
1789

COMPROMISE OF 1850
OREGON TERRITORY
MINNESOTA TERRITORY
UNORGANIZED TERRITORY
UTAH TERRITORY
NEW MEXICO TERRITORY
MISSOURI COMPROMISE LINE
IOWA
WIS.
MICH.
ILL.
IND.
OHIO
MO.
KY.
TENN.
ARK.
MISS.
ALA.
GA.
LA.
FLA.
TEXAS
VA.
N.C.
S.C.
MAINE
N.H.
VT.
MA.
N.Y.
R.I.
CONN.
N.J.
DEL.
MD.
MASON-DIXON LINE
Free states and territories
Slave states

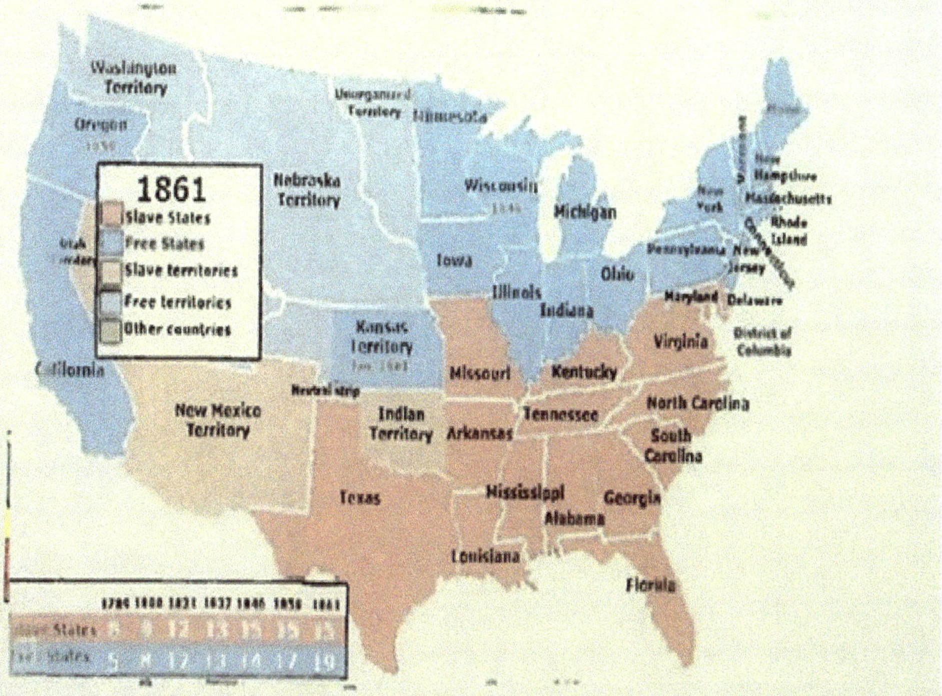
1861
Slave States
Free States
Slave territories
Free territories
Other countries
Washington Territory
Oregon
Unorganized Territory
Minnesota
Nebraska Territory
Wisconsin
Michigan
Iowa
Illinois
Indiana
Ohio
Kansas Territory
California
New Mexico Territory
Neutral strip
Indian Territory
Missouri
Kentucky
Tennessee
Arkansas
Texas
Mississippi
Alabama
Georgia
Louisiana
Florida
Virginia
North Carolina
South Carolina
Maryland
Delaware
District of Columbia
Pennsylvania
New Jersey
New York
New Hampshire
Massachusetts
Rhode Island
1789 1800 1821 1837 1846 1858 1861

CHAPTER FIVE

Willie Lynch Slave Speech 1712 And Making of a Slave

William Lynch aka Willie Lynch, a British citizen slave owner in the Caribbean traveled to Virginia in 1712 to purportedly deliver a speech on the banks of the James River regarding control of slaves in the colonies, before a group of slave owners. Willie Lynch identifies himself as the master of a "modest plantation" in the British West Indies who has been summoned to the Virginia colony by local slaveowners to advise them on problems they have been having in managing their slaves. He briefly notes that their current violent method of handling unruly slaves -lynching (though the term is not used or even invented at this time) is inefficient and counterproductive. Instead, he suggests that they adopt his method, which consists of exploiting differences such as age, and skin color in order to pit slaves against each other. This method, he assures his hosts will "control the slaves for at least 300 years, Embree, E.R. (1931). The term "lynching" is believed to be attributed to William Lynch by other years later. The speech was relatively short but effective.

THE SPEECH

Greetings. "Gentlemen I greet you here on the James River in the year of our Lord one thousand seven hundred and twelve. First, I shall thank you, the gentlemen of the Colony of Virginia, for bringing me here. I am here to help you solve some of your problems with slaves. Your invitation reached me on my modest plantation in the West Indies, where I have experimented with some of the newest and still the oldest methods for control of slaves. Ancient Rome would envy us if my program is implemented. As our boat sailed south on the James River, named for our illustrious king, whose version of the Bible we Cherish, I saw enough to know that your problem is not unique. While Rome used cords of wood as crosses for standing human bodies along it's highways in great numbers, you are here using the tree and the rope on occasion. I caught the whiff of a dead slave hanging from a tree, a couple miles back. You are only losing valuable stock by hangings, you are having uprisings, slaves are running away, your crops are sometimes left in the fields too long for maximum profit, you suffer occasional fires, your animals are killed. Gentlemen, you know what your problems are; I do not need to elaborate. I am not here to enumerate your problems; I am here to introduce you to a method of solving them. In my bag here, I HAVE A FULL PROOF METHOD FOR CONTROLLING YOUR BLACK SLAVES. I guarantee every one of you that if installed properly IT WILL CONTROL THE SLAVES FOR AT LEAST THREE HUNDRED YEARS. My method is simple. Any member of your family or overseer can use it. I HAVE OUTLINED A NUMBER OF DIFFERENCES AMONG THE SLAVES; AND I TAKE THESE DIFFERENCES AND MAKE THEM BIGGER. I USE FEAR, DISTRUST AND ENVY FOR CONTROL PURPOSES. These methods have worked on my modest plantation in the West Indies, and it will work throughout the South. Take this simple little list of differences and think about them. On top of my list is "AGE". The second is "COLOR" or shade, there is INTELLEGENCE, SIZE, SEX, SIZES OF PLANTATIONS, STATUS on plantations, ATTITUDE of owners, whether the slaves live in the valley, on a hill, East, West, North, South, have fine hair, course hair, or is tall or short. Now that you have a list of differences, I shall give you an outline of action, but before that, I shall assure you that DISTRUST IS STRONGER THAN TRUST AND ENVY IS SLAVES TRUST AND DEPEND ON US. THEY MUST LOVE, RESPECT AND TRUST ONLY US. Gentlemen these kits are your keys to control. Use them. Have your wives and children use them, never miss an opportunity. IF USED INTENSELY FOR ONE YEAR, THE SLAVES THEMSELVES WILL REMAIN PERPETUALLY DISTRUSTFUL. Thank you, gentlemen."

Disclosure: This speech has been extracted from several sources listed in the references and will be included in a comprehensive treatise on the issue and history of slavery in America and Africa as well as the subject of slave ownership by American Blacks and Indians before the Civil War; in my next book: Black and Red: Negro and Native American SLAVE OWNERS in North America 1651-1865. Colonel Vaughan Witten PhD.

REFERENCES

Willie Lynch Letter: The making of a slave. Final Call.com news,(2009)
Farrakhan, Louis. An Appeal...www. Millionsmore movement.com,(2005)
Rosenzweig, Roy. The Road to Zanadu: Public and private pathway history 2001.
Taylor, C. (2007) Slave consultant narra. Links: Missisippi Black Codes 1865.
Fredrick Douglass-Life as a slave in America, (Virginia.edu)

Now the details of how to make a slave by Willie Lynch. You're not going to like it but...we can't deny reality no matter how horrible and despicable. So here goes: Willie Lynch

"LET'S MAKE A SLAVE"

What do we need? First of all, we need a black nigger man, a pregnant nigger woman and her baby nigger boy. Second, we will use the same basic principle that we use in breaking a horse, combined with some more sustaining factors. We reduce them from their natural state in nature; whereas nature provides them with the natural capacity to take care of their needs and the needs of their offspring, we break that natural string of independence from them and thereby create a dependency state so that we may be able to get from them useful production for our business and pleasure.

CARDINAL PRINCIPLES FOR MAKING A NEGRO:

For fear that our future generations may not understand the principle of breaking horses and men, we lay down the art. For if we are to sustain our basic economy, we must break both of the beasts together, the nigger and the horse. We understand that short range planning in economics results in economic chaos, so that, to avoid turmoil in the economy, it requires us to have breadth and depth in long range comprehensive planning, articulating both skill and sharp perception. We lay down the following principles for long range comprehensive economic planning.

(1) Both horses and niggers are no good to the economy in the wild or natural state.
(2) Both must be broken and tied together for orderly production.
(3) For orderly futures, special and particular attention must be paid to the female and the youngest offspring.
(4) Both must be crossbred to produce a variety and division of labor.
(5) Both must be taught to respond to a peculiar new language.
(6) Psychological and physical instruction of containment must be created for both.

We hold the above six cardinal principles as truths to be self-evident, based upon the following discourse concerning the economics of breaking and tying the horse and nigger together...all inclusive of the six principles laid down above.

Note: Neither principle alone will suffice for good economics. All principles must be employed for the orderly good of the nation. Accordingly, both a wild horse or natural nigger is dangerous even if captured, for they will have the tendency to seek their customary freedom, and, in doing so might kill you in your sleep. You cannot rest. They sleep while you are awake and are awake while you sleep. They are dangerous near the family house, and it requires too much labor to watch them away from the house. Above all you cannot get them to work in this natural state. Hence, both the horse and the nigger must be bro ken, that is to take them from one form of mental life to another, keep the body and take the mind. In other words, break the will to resist.

Now the breaking process is the same for the horse and the nigger, only slightly varying in degrees. But as we said before, you must keep your focused eye on the female and the offspring of the horse and the nigger. A brief discourse in offspring development will shed light on the key economic principles. If you break the female, she will break the offspring in its early years of development, and when the offspring is old enough to work, she will deliver it up to you. For example, take the stud horse, break him for limited containment. Completely break the female horse until she becomes very gentle whereas anybody can ride in comfort. Breed the mare until you have the desired offspring. Then you can turn the stud out to freedom until you need him again. Train the female horse whereby she will eat out of you hand, and she will train the infant horse to eat out of your hand also.

When it comes to breaking the uncivilized nigger, use the same process, but vary the degree and step up the pressure, so as to do a complete reversal of the mind. Take the meanest and most restless nigger, strip him of his clothes in front of the remaining niggers, the female and the offspring, tar and feather him, tie his legs to two horses faced in different directions, set him on fire and beat both horses to pull him apart in front of the remaining niggers. The next step is to take a bull whip and beat the remaining nigger males to the point of near death in front of the females and infants. Don't kill him. But put the fear of God in him, for he can be useful for future breeding.

THE BREAKING PROCESSING OF THE AFRICAN WOMAN

Take the female and run a series of tests on her to see if she will submit to your desires willingly. Test her in every way, because she is the most important factor for good economics. If she shows any signs of resistance, use the bull whip to extract the last bit of bitch out of her. Take care not to kill her, for to do so, you spoil good economics.

When in complete submission, she will train her offspring in the early years to submit to labor when they become of age. Understanding is the best thing. By this breaking of the female nigger, we have reversed the relationship. In her natural uncivilized state, she would have a strong dependency on the uncivilized nigger male, and she would have a limited protective dependency toward her independent male offspring and would raise female offspring to be dependent like her. Nature had provided for this balance. We reversed nature by burning and pulling apart the male nigger and bull whipping the other males in her presence. By her being left alone, unprotected, with the male image destroyed, the ordeal caused her to move from her psychological dependent state to a frozen independent state. In this state she will raise her male and female offspring in reversed roles. Nigger females being, without influence of the nigger male image, frozen with an independent psychology will raise her boy to be weak and dependent, but physically strong, in other words, body over mind. We will mate and breed them and continue the cycle. By reversing the positions of the male and female savages, we created an orbital cycle that turns on its axis forever; unless a phenomenon occurred, and reshifted the positions of the male and female savages. Our experts warned us that it was possible for this phenomenon to occur. They say the mind has a strong drive to correct and re-correct itself over a period of time it can touch some substantial original historical basis, and they advised us that the best way to deal with this phenomenon is shave off the brute's mental history and create a multiplicity of illusions so that each illusion would twill in its own orbit, to create a diversified division of labor. The result of which is severance of points of beginning of each illusion. To do this required cross breeding of the nigger and the horse. Cross breeding of the horse means taking a horse and breeding it with an ass, and you get a dumb backward ass, long headed mule that is not productive or reproductive by itself. Cross breeding niggers means taking so many drops of good white blood, varying the drops by the various tone that you want, then let them breed with each other until the cycle of colors appear as you desire. You got a multiplicity of colors of ass backwards, unusual niggers, running, tied to backwards long headed mules, the one being productive of itself, the other being sterile. (The one constant, the other dying. We keep the nigger constant, for we may replace the mule with another tool) both nigger and mule tied to each other, neither knowing where the other came from and neither productive for itself, nor without each other.

CONTROLLED LANGUAGE

Crossbreeding completed, for further severance from their original beginning, we must completely annihilate the mother tongue of the nigger and the new mule and institute a new language that involves the new life's work of both. Language is a peculiar institution. It leads to the heart of people.

The more a foreigner knows about the language of another country, the more he is able to move through all levels of their society.

Therefore, if the foreigner is an enemy of a country, to the extent that he knows the body of the language, to that extent is the country vulnerable to attack or invasion of a foreign culture. For example, you take the slave, if you teach him all about your language, he will know your secrets, and then he is no longer a slave, for you can't fool him any longer, and having a fool is one of the basic ingredients of and incident to the making of the slavery system.

By the Black Arcade Liberation Library; 1970. (Recompiled and reedited by Kenneth T. Spann. 1997-2003 Information Man, Inc.)

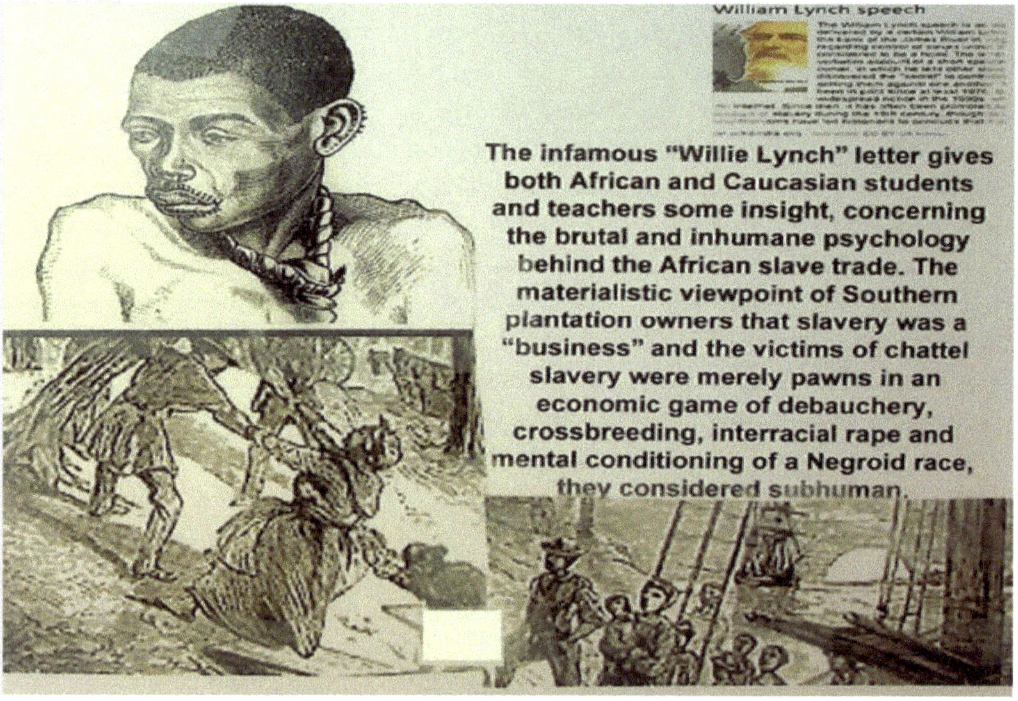
William Lynch speech
The infamous "Willie Lynch" letter gives both African and Caucasian students and teachers some insight, concerning the brutal and inhumane psychology behind the African slave trade. The materialistic viewpoint of Southern plantation owners that slavery was a "business" and the victims of chattel slavery were merely pawns in an economic game of debauchery, crossbreeding, interracial rape and mental conditioning of a Negroid race, they considered subhuman.

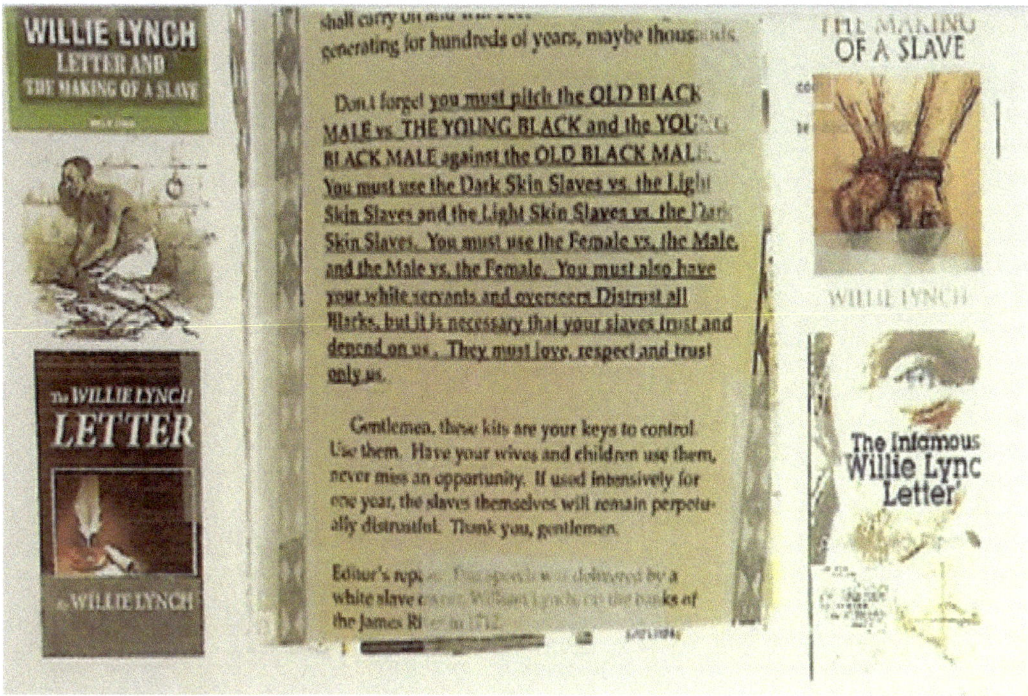
WILLIE LYNCH
LETTER AND
THE MAKING OF A SLAVE
The WILLIE LYNCH
LETTER
WILLIE LYNCH
Don't forget you must pitch the OLD BLACK MALE vs. THE YOUNG BLACK and the YOUNG BLACK MALE against the OLD BLACK MALE.
You must use the Dark Skin Slaves vs. the Light Skin Slaves and the Light Skin Slaves vs. the Dark Skin Slaves. You must use the Female vs. the Male, and the Male vs. the Female. You must also have your white servants and overseers Distrust all Blacks, but it is necessary that your slaves trust and depend on us. They must love, respect and trust only us.
Gentlemen, these kits are your keys to control. Use them. Have your wives and children use them, never miss an opportunity. If used intensively for one year, the slaves themselves will remain perpetually distrustful. Thank you, gentlemen.
OF A SLAVE
WILLIE LYNCH
The Infamous
Willie Lync
Letter

Chapter Six

Anthony Johnson and John Casor

Anthony Johnson 1600-1670 was a Black Angolan who achieved freedom in the early 17th century in the colony of Virginia after serving his term of indenture. He became a property owner and was one of the first people in Virginia to have his right to own a slave legally recognized. Held as an indentured servant inl621, he earned his freedom after several years, and was granted land by the colony, Foner, Philip. S (1980).

He later became a successful farmer in Maryland. He attained great wealth after having been an indentured servant.

Johnson was captured in his native Angola by an enemy tribe and sold to Arab slave traders. He was eventually sold as an indentured servant to a merchant working for the Virginia company, Horton, (2002). He arrived in Virginia in 1621 on the JAMES. The Virginia muster (census) of 1624 lists his name as "Antonio, name not given" and recorded as a "Negro".

Johnson was sold to a white planter named Bennet as an indentured servant to work on his tobacco farm. Servants typically worked under an indenture contract for four to seven years to pay off their passage, room, board, lodging, and freedom dues. In the early colonial years, most Africans in the Thirteen Colonies were held under such contracts of indentured servitude. They were typically released after a contracted period with many of the indentured receiving land and equipment after their contracts expired or were bought out.

In 1623, his future wife arrived. "Mary, a Negro" arrived from England aboard the ship MARGARET. She was brought to work on the same plantation as Antonio, where she was the only woman. Antonio and Mary married and lived together for 40 years, Breen, (1980). Sometime around 1635 Antonio and Mary gained their freedom from indenture. Antonio changed his name to Anthony Johnson and enters the legal record as a free man when he purchased a calf in 1647. Johnson was granted a large plot of farmland after he paid off his indentured contract with his labor. In 1651 he acquired 250 acres under the "head right system" by buying the contracts of five indentured servants, one being his son, Richard, - Heinegg, Paul. (2005). The five contracts were for one white and four blacks including a John Casor.

In 1653, John Casor felt his contract of servitude was up. Having been contracted, "employed", by Johnson for 7 or 8 years, Casor demanded to be freed. Initially Johnson refused but relented after encouragement from his wife. Casor went on to work for planter Richard Parker and his brother George under an indentured contract. Under the headright system, each new person in the colony was afforded 50 acres of land. For an indentured servant, that land went to his employer until the contract of servitude was up. Fearing that the colony would take back his lands if his servants ended their contracts, he, Johnson sued Robert Parker for illegally detaining his Negro servant. Parker and his brother George, testified that Casor came to him as a freed indentured servant, while Johnson took the position that he had Casor for life. Johnson initially lost his case but appealed and the North Hampton County court eventually favored and sided with Johnson, and Casor became his servant for life, spending the remainder of his years as the first slave declared via civil litigation. Earlier in 1640, an African, John Punch was ordered into lifetime slavery, but his sentence was a punishment under criminal law for escaping from his master, in sustaining the claim of Johnson to the perpetual service of Casor, the court also gave judicial sanction to the right of Negros to own slaves of their own race, Russell, John H. (1916). After this 1653- 1655 court case, legal restrictions continued to be made related to African servants. The courts likely reasoned "In so far as Negros were heathens, they could never become Englishmen; in so as they could never become Englishmen, they could not be entitled to the protection of the common law", which at the time was limited to English subjects, Wood, William J. (1970). Africans were considered foreigners or aliens.

In 1662, the colony passed a law that children of enslaved women (who were of African descent and - thus foreigners) were to take the status of the mother, rather than the father, as was current under English common law. This principle called Partus Sequitur Ventrum was adopted from Roman law, Banks, T. L. (2009). Under this law, children born of a free white mother and Negro father were born free. In 1691, the law was amended; such mixed-race children had to serve as an indentured servant for 30 years while the mother would be fined 15 pounds sterling. If the mother failed to pay the fine, within a month of birth she was indentured herself for 5 years, Slavery and Indentured Servants, Law Library of Congress (2017). By an act in 1699, the colony ordered all free Blacks deported, virtually defining as slaves all persons of African descent as slaves who remained in the colony, Wood, William, (1970).

THE FIRST SLAVE OWNER IN AMERICA WAS NOT ONLY A BLACK MAN, HE WENT TO COURT AND DEMANDED IT
IN 1654, IT WAS TIME FOR ANTHONY TO RELEASE JOHN CASOR, A BLACK INDENTURED SERVANT. INSTEAD ANTHONY TOLD CASOR HE WAS EXTENDING HIS TIME. CASOR LEFT AND BECAME EMPLOYED BY THE FREE WHITE MAN ROBERT PARKER.
ANTHONY JOHNSON SUED ROBERT PARKER IN THE NORTHAMPTON COURT IN 1654. IN 1655, THE COURT RULED THAT ANTHONY JOHNSON COULD HOLD JOHN CASOR INDEFINITELY. THE COURT GAVE JUDICIAL SANCTION FOR BLACKS TO OWN A SLAVE OF THEIR OWN RACE. THUS CASOR BECAME THE FIRST PERMANENT SLAVE AND JOHNSON THE FIRST SLAVE OWNER.
POLITICAL CORRECTNESS MUST DIE
Anthony Johnson the pioneer of American slavery
John CASOR -CASTOR
JOHNSONS FIRST SLAVE
ANTHONY JOHNSON - SLAVE OWNER

CHAPTER SEVEN

Slavery by BLACK Slave Owners

Robert M. Grooms in " The Johnson Family: African American Owners of White and Black Slaves" has revealed the fact that Blacks owned White slaves in America. He also notes that a legal precedent for life-long slavery in America was established by a Black slave owner with regard to one of his Black slaves.

"On April 10, 1606, the Virginia company of London was granted a royal charter by King James I, awarding a tract of land in present day Virginia, Delaware and Maryland, Ironbark Resources, (2013)."

On May 13, 1607, three small ships, Susan Constant, Godspeed and Discovery arrived at Cape Henry, sailed up the James River, and landed at present day Jamestown. Following a 131-day voyage crowded in damp, cold, foul smelling holds in the darkness beneath the decks, 104 settlers including 12 servants, disembarked and established a rough log fortress, (IBID).

In August 1619, more than a year before the landing of the ship Mayflower, a captured Dutch man-of-war with a Spanish captain named Jope and an English pilot named Marmaduke, anchored in the James River near Jamestown. On board were "20 and odd" men and women of African descent. The Virginia colony was in need of laborers, while the captain and his crew were in need of supplies. A bargain was struct and 20 Negros, the first of their race in the colonies, were sold to the colonists, fresh food and water was brought aboard, and the ship sailed away, (IBID).

According to Duke University history professor, Dr. John Hope Franklin: These newcomers who happened to be Black, were simply more indentured servants. They were listed in the census counts of 1623 and 1624; and as late as 1651, Negros whose period of service had expired, had also being assigned land much the same way that it was being assigned to whites who had completed their indenture.

In 1651, Anthony Johnson (a Negro) was given 250 acres as "head rights" for purchasing five incoming redemptioners, (that is passengers who had to work off their debt of travel, food, board and freedom dues to their New World masters, as indentured servants for 7 to 10 years. In 1652 slaveowner Anthony Johnson's eldest son, purchased eleven c incoming white males and females, and received 550 acres adjacent to his father, Grooms, Robert, M. (1995). The redemptioners were typically whites who voluntarily came to America with the contract promise to pay their debt via indentured servitude, whereas the African Blacks were captives destined to pay also but not voluntarily. In either case in the early days, they received 250 acres of land once their contracted time expired. There were a number of additional Virginia land patents representing grants to free Blacks of from 50 to 550 acres for purchasing redemptioners, or persons who would redeem their debt with 7 to 10 years of labor. For example, on April 1667 Emanuel Cabew received 50 acres in James City County, and in 1668 fifty acres were deeded to John Harris of Queens Creek. Francis Payne paid for his freedom in 1650 by purchasing three incoming whites for his master, (IBID). Blacks and Indians came to own, and abuse, whites in Virginia in such large numbers that in 1670 the House of Burgesses (legislature) proclaimed that" noe negro or Indian that though baptized and enjoyed their own freedom shall be capable of any purchase of Christians, but yet not be debarred from buying any of their own nation"." Christian" was a euphemism for Caucasian. Virginia's Slave Code of 1705 provided: "That no negros, mulattos, Indians, although Christians, ore Jew, Moore, Mahhometans,or other infidels, shall at any time purchase any Christian, nor any other, except of their own complexion, or such as are declared slaves by this act", (IBID).

The census of 1830 lists 935 free Black slave owners in Louisiana, owning 4,206 slaves. The state of South Carolina lists 464 free Blacks owning 2,715 slaves, Tremoglie, Michael, P "The Black Roots of Slavery". In 1860 there were at least six Negros in Louisiana who owned 65 or more slaves. The largest number, 152 slaves, were owned by the widow C. Richards and her son who owned a large sugar cane plantation.

Henry Koger in "Black slave owners in South Carolina reports that," 1860 so many Black women in Charleston had inherited or been given slaves and other property by white men , and used their property to start successful businesses, that they owned 70% of the Black owned slaves in the city, Vogeler, Ingolf, (1985).

From Koger's work it is noted that free Black slave owners resided in states as north as New York and as far south as Florida, extending westward into Kentucky, Mississippi, Louisiana, and Missouri. According to the federal census of 1830 free Blacks owned more than 10,000 slaves in Louisiana, Maryland, South Carolina, and Virginia. The majority of Black slave owners lived in Louisiana and planted sugar cane, (IBID).

The majority of slave owners, white and Black owned only one to five slaves, and the mean wealth of the southern white man in 1860 was $3,978, (IBID).

CHAPTER EIGHT

SLAVERY BY NATIVE AMERICAN INDIAN OWNERS

Black slavery in America usually evokes images of the antebellum South, but few realize that members of the Five Civilized Tribes—the Cherokees, Choctaws, Chickasaws, Creeks and Seminoles in Indian Territory, todays Oklahoma, also had slaves, Burton, A. T. (1996). Like their counterparts in the South, Indian slave holders feared slave revolts. Those fears came true in 1842 when the slaves in the Cherokee Nation made a daring dash for freedom, (IBID).

In the 1830s and 1840s, initially at the insistence of President Andrew Jackson, the United States government forcibly removed the Five Civilized Tribes from their homes in Mississippi, Alabama, Tennessee, North Carolina, Georgia, and Florida to Indian Territory west of the Mississippi River. Their removal opened the lands to white settlers and planters. When they moved, all the tribes took with them established systems of slavery. Mixed-blood Indians, the offspring of white traders and frontiersmen who married Indian women, were the principal slave holders in the tribes, largely because their fathers had taught them the economics of slavery. Those mixed-blood Indians remained tribal members and became important middlemen between white settlers and Indian communities, (IBID). Many Cherokees depended on black slaves as a bridge to white society. Full-blooded Indian slave owners relied on the blacks as English interpreters and translators.

By 1840, the Cherokees had 4,600 slaves; the Choctaws, 2,344; the Creeks, 1,532; the Chickasaws, 975; and the Seminoles, 500. Some Indian slave holders were as harsh and cruel as any white slave master. Indians were often hired to catch runaway slaves; in fact, slavecatching was a lucrative way of life for some Indians, especially the Chickasaws, (IBID).

Seminoles' attitudes toward slavery were different than those of other tribes. Never practicing in chattel slavery, they took in fugitive slaves and claimed them as their own "property" to protect the Blacks from slave catchers. In return, the Blacks, who lived in separate villages in the Seminole country, gave livestock and crops to the Indians. The Blacks and Seminoles also formed a military alliance, with Blacks serving the Indians as warriors and strategists. In some instances, the Blacks would intermarry into the Seminole community. All the tribes except the Seminoles had slave codes. Even after their removal to Indian Territory, the Seminoles allowed their slaves to carry weapons and own horses and other property. In 1849, tired of harassment from slave catchers, some of the free Black Seminoles under Black Chief John Horse fled the Indian Territory. They joined Seminole Chief Wild Cat and his followers and made it to Mexico.

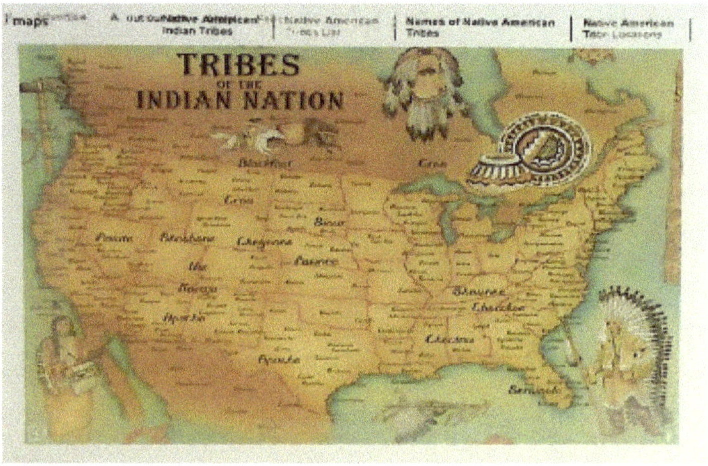

By 1851, nearly 300 Blacks had tried to escape from Indian Territory, most headed for Mexico or Kansas. In the northern Cherokee nation, in what would later become Washington County, Oklahoma, the "underground railroad" trail led into Kansas. None of the escapes, however, equaled the scope of the Cherokee slave revolt of 1842. The Cherokees thought the influence of "foreign" free Blacks had caused the slave insurrection. On December 2, 1842, they passed "An Act in Regard to Free Negros" directing that all free Blacks, except those whom Cherokees had freed, leave the Cherokee Nation by January 1, 1843, or as soon after as possible. Those who lingered or refused would be expelled. The act targeted free Black Seminoles living in the Cherokee Nation, (IBID).

The conclusion of this chapter reveals an unfortunate truth that the Cherokees have recently harmed the descendants of the slaves they held in the 1800s. As recent as 2011 the Cherokee nation booted out from membership the thousands of slave descendants that they had admitted into their tribe when they came to Oklahoma in the 1840s. This was done by a tribal Supreme Court ruling, Johnson, C. & McCune, G. (2011), Reuters. According to Steve Olafson, (2011), the motivation stemmed from a controversy about a footnote in the brutal history of the U.S. treatment of Native Americans. When many Indians were forced to move to what later became Oklahoma, from the eastern U.S. in 1838, some who had owned plantations in the south, brought along their slaves. Some 4,000 Indians died during the forced march, which became known as the "Trail of Tears". Marilyn Vann, the Freedman leader who is the plaintiff in the legal battle, claims that this decision "Is racism and apartheid in the 21st century". The decision to exclude the Freedmen also rankled some African American members of Congress, which has jurisdiction over all Native American tribes in the country. A lawsuit challenging the Freedmen's removal from the tribe has been pending in federal court in Washington, for about six years, (IBID).

As a sovereign nation, Cherokee officials maintain that the tribe has the right to amend its constitutional membership requirements. Removal from the tribe membership means the Freedman will no longer be eligible for health benefits.

Chapter Nine

Impact of Slavery on American Blacks

In some ways enslaved African American families very much resembled other families who lived in other times and places and under vastly different circumstances. Some husbands and wives loved each other; some did not get along. Children sometimes abided by their parents' rules; other times they followed their own minds. Most parents loved their children and wanted to protect them. In some critical ways, though, the slavery that marked everything about their lives made these families very different. Belonging to another human being brought unique constrictions, disruptions, frustrations and pain, Williams, H. A., (2017). Enslaved people could not legally marry in any American colony or state. Colonial and state laws considered them property and commodities, not legal persons who could enter into contracts, and marriage was, and is, very much a legal contract, (IBID). This means that until 1865 when slavery ended in this country, the majority of African Americans could not legally marry. In northern states such as New York, Pennsylvania, or Massachusetts, where slavery had ended by 1830, free African Americans could marry, but in the slave states of the South, many enslaved people entered into relationships that they treated like marriage; they considered themselves husbands and wives even though they knew that their unions were not protected by state law, (IBID).

Some enslaved people lived in nuclear families with a mother, father, and children. In these cases, each family member belonged to the same owner. Others lived in near- nuclear families in which the father had a different owner than the mother and children. Both slaves and slave owners referred to these relationships as "abroad marriages", (IBID). A father might live several miles away on a distant plantation and walk, usually on Wednesday nights and Saturday evenings to see his family as his obligation to provide labor for an owner, took precedence over his personal needs, (IBID).

This use of unpaid labor to produce wealth lay at the heart of slavery in America. Enslaved people usually worked from early in the morning until late at night. Women often returned to work shortly after giving birth, sometimes running from the fields during the day to feed their infants. On large plantations or farms, it was common for children to come under the care of one enslaved woman who was designated to feed and watch over them during the day while their parents worked. By the time most enslaved children reached the age of seven or eight they were also assigned tasks including taking care of owner's young children, fanning flies from the table, running errands, taking lunch to owners children at school, and eventually working in the tobacco, cotton, corn, or rice fields along with the adults.

In the large plantations, in the slave quarters, they were somewhat removed from the scrutiny of the owners, overseers and patrollers. The slaves held parties and prayer meetings in the woods beyond the hearing of whites. Parents also taught children lessons on loyalty, how to treat people and stories about their ancestors. The slaves lived with the perpetual possibility of separation through the sale of one or more of the family members. Slaves were valuable and traded or sold as commodities in financial transactions or at death of the owner, as part of the estate transfer.

Paradoxically, despite the likelihood of breaking up the family, family formation actually helped owners keep slavery in place. Many masters reasoned that having families made it less likely that a man or woman would run away, which would break up their family and reduce the loss of valuable property. Many owners encouraged marriage and the ritual of "jumping the broom", even sometimes giving them gifts. Just as owners used the formation of family ties to their own advantage, abolitionists used the specter of separation to argue against the institution of slavery.

Following the Civil War, when slavery finally ended in America after nearly 250 years, former slaves took measures to formalize their family relations by legally marrying their partner, looking for their children that had been sold away and get them from their former owner, and using newspaper advertisements to find members of their families.

There is no question that a weakened Black family emerged from slavery. The destruction of the family unit through the intrusion of the slave master's sexual exploitation of women and other evil designs evolved into a volatile moral code of Black people, (IBID).

It is believed by many scholars and politicians that this has led to the consequence today that over 70% of African American children are born to unmarried women in America, and as a result such large numbers of children born to single mothers is clearly a wrong model for a stable, secure future for Black people, and establishes a link between an absent father and high school drop outs and criminal behavior, Atlanta Black Star. Com., (2013).

Food: The diets of many Black people in present America are a direct result of slavery. The slave masters generally consumed the lean and fleshy parts of farm animals and left the scraps for the enslaved. Enslaved Africans were forced to incorporate those leftovers such as tripe, pig feet, chitterlings, oxtails, cow foot, and other bad foods-into their daily meals. Those unhealthy foods are still part of the diets of many Black people today. They are harmful to the body and are the main cause of chronic illnesses that plague our communities including strokes, high blood pressure, diabetes, and heart disease, PBS.org. (2013).

Self-Hate: The slave masters used Machiavellian (devious, cunning, unscrupulous) systems to mentally break the enslaved Africans. While validating themselves as superior, they used every propaganda tool within their power to teach Black people to hate themselves. The results still have major impact on the psyche of Black people today, digitalhistory.uh.edu. (2013).

ANALYSIS & CONCLUSION REGARDING THE PURPORTED IMPACT OF SLAVERY ON THE AMERICAN BLACK POPULATION

Iit would seem obvious and apparent to most clear, unbiased, even semi-literate, “”normal thinking” people will conceive of and admit to the concept that the 250 years of cruel, brutal, inhuman practice of slavery perpetrated and executed on the African people brought here against their will; had a profound psychological and cultural effect on the Freed slaves and would manifest itself for generations in their behavior, psyche, trust level and their general world view. However - even when presented with the evidence presented and referenced in the previous chapters-one must question whether the outrageous, anti-social irreverent and unlawful behavior of our young Black males in particular and to a lesser extent Black females, can be justified and or explained by invoking the past treatment of slavery and the prediction of Willie Lynch, that his methodology would control us (Negros/Blacks) for 300 years after 1712, and maybe for 1000 years. Yes, I agree that it has affected us, but after 152 years of freedom, even with discrimination, we should be able to throw off our psychological chains as well as the physical chains of 1619 to 1865. In order to investigate this phenomenon, we must look at the major variables involved in our history since 1865 and the possible effects on our behavior as a result of the earlier 246 years of oppression and slavery.

The generally accepted areas of inquiry regarding differential components and variables guiding and or controlling group success and adaptation to a particular situation or culture can be boiled down to one of the following hypotheses.

1. That the failed group lack's ability, natural intelligence, and are incapable of adapting and assimilating into a particular society.

2. That the failed group is sufficiently restricted and restrained in their efforts to adapt, by institutional laws, conventions, and practices.

3. That the individual behavior of the group is anti-social, criminal and anti-ethical to the folkways, conventions, mores and laws of the particular society.

Ways Slavery Affected Black Families And Still Has An Impact Today

By **Yanique Dawkins** - October 13, 2014

Broken Traditions

African family traditions, which varied according to national origin and religion, could not be replicated in the New World after Africans were forced into slavery. The slave trade was responsible for breaking up African families. Husbands, wives and children could be sold separately because U.S. law did not legally recognize their families.

Broken Families

Enslaved Black people were denied a secure family life. Because they were property and could not legally marry, a permanent family could not be a guaranteed part of enslaved people's lives. They had no right to live or stay together, no right to their own children, and it was common for enslaved parents and children to live apart.

In this regard I will address each of these hypotheses as to the degree they fit into this paradigm and select the one that best explains our (Black) experience and lack of success in America.

HYPOTHESIS #1 Lack of Ability and Intelligence to Learn & Adapt.

The connection between race and intelligence has been a subject of debate in both popular science and academic research since the inception of IQ testing in the early 20th century. While tests have broadly shown differences in average scores based on self

-identified race, there is considerable debate as to whether (and to what extent) those differences reflect environmental or biological factors. As a point of reference, it has been strongly documented that Blacks in America have a negative 15-point difference in IQ scores, a 1 standard deviation on the standard average score of 100. Currently there is no non-circumstantial evidence that the differences in test scores have a genetic component, McIntosh, 2011, pp. 358. Intelligence is a polygenetic trait. This means that intelligence is under the influence of several genes, possibly several thousand, and it is generally conceptualized as the ability to reason, solve problems and adapt to the environment, Plomin, Kennedy, & Craig, 2005, pp. 513.

Howard Gardner, of Harvard School of Education has identified nine types of intelligence:

NATURALISIC INTELLENCE (Nature Smart), which designates the human ability to discriminate among living things (plants, animals) as well as sensitivity to other features of the natural world. This ability was clearly of value in our evolutionary past as hunters, gatherers, and farmers. It continues to be applicable to our "natural environment" in our ability to discriminate among cars, sneakers, houses, animals, and the like. Blacks appear to be competent in this area and thus PASS on this intelligence.

MUSICAL INTELLIGENCE, (Musical Smart) Musical intelligence is the capacity to discern pitch, rhythm, timbre, and tone. This intelligence enables us to recognize, create, reproduce, and reflect on music as demonstrated by conductors, vocalists, musicians and sensitive listeners; also singers as well as making a connection between music and emotion. Blacks are outstanding in this arena as well as dancing. I give Blacks a PASS as well on this factor of intelligence.

LOGICAL-MATHEMATICAL INTELLIGENCE Logical- Mathematical intelligence is the ability to calculate, quantify, consider propositions and hypotheses, and carry out complete mathematical operations. It enables us to perceive relationships and connections and use abstract, symbolic thought; sequential reasoning skills; and inductive and deductive thinking patterns. Blacks FAIL in this area.

EXISTENTIAL INTELLENCE is the sensitivity and capacity to tackle deep questions about human existence, such as the meaning of life, why we die, and how did we get here. Blacks PASS in this area.

INTERPERSONAL INTELLIGENCE (PEOPLE SMART) is the ability to understand and interact effectively with others. It involves effective verbal and nonverbal communication, the ability to note distinctions among others, sensitivity to the moods and temperaments of others, and the ability to entertain multiple perspectives. BLACKS FAIL in this area.

BODILY - KINESTHETIC INTELLIGENCE (Body Smart) is the ability and capacity to manipulate objects and use a variety of physical skills. This intelligence also involves a sense of timing and the perfection of skills through mind and body union.

Athletes, dancers and surgeons typically possess this intelligence. BLACKS PASS at a very high level here, especially in dancing and athletics.

LINGUISTC INTELLIGENCE is the ability to think and use language to express and appreciate complex meanings and understand the order and meaning of words. Young adults with this intelligence enjoy reading and writing. BLACKS FAIL in this area by a wide margin. There is a widely held belief that "if you want to keep a secret from a Black person, WRITE IT DOWN."

INTRA-PERSONAL INTELLIGENCE (Self Smart) is the capacity to understand oneself, thoughts and feelings in planning and directing one's life, and an appreciation of the self and the human condition. BLACKS FAIL in this area.

SPATIAL INTELLIGENCE is the ability to think in three dimensions. Core capacities include mental imagery, spatial reasoning, image manipulation and graphic skills. BLACKS FAIL here also.

AUTHOR'S NOTE: The different intelligence type descriptions in this section is attributed to Howard Gardner (2011), but the assignment of PASS-FAIL assessment is mine: Colonel V. Witten.

Even though Blacks score a complete standard deviation score of 15 points below Whites, their intellectual capabilities spread over the nine types of Dr Gardner appears to be sufficient to eliminate hypothesis #1 Lack of Intelligence and ability to Learn as the basic reason for failure. ERGO REJECT HYP. #1.

Types of Intelligence

This part of our website will be concentrating on trying to define or catagorize intelligence. As you can imagine, this is potentially a very difficult process since the world is not constituted of one aspect of life. That is to say that if everyone in the world worked for one thing, let s just say being the world's best weight lifter, there would only be one type of person in the world. We could either categorize an individual as being a good weight lifter or a bad weightlifter. Fortunately that is not how the world works; so you see, this is what makes today's categorizing of intellect so difficult. One person may be a carpenter and be excellent at working with wood; another person may be a physics professor and be excellent at remembering formulas, and figuring out mathematical relationships. I would say that both of these people are intelligent, in their own way But what does "in their own way" mean, and how can we catagorize someone's intelligence?

Left vs. Right

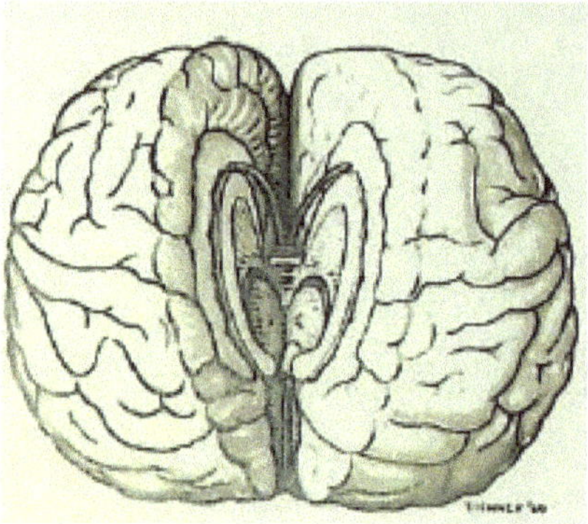

Let's start out by cutting one category of intelligence into two; Left and Right brain. You may have heard someone tell you that they are more "left-brained" than "right-brained". What does this mean? Our brains are structurally/physically split into two separates halves by the corpus callosum. This physical boundary sets up a nice way to describe the brain; left versus right side. It is known that the differing sides of the brain perform different functions. For example, for 95% of right-handed people, the area in the brain that is in charge of speech is located on the left half of the brain. Compiling all of the specilized functions to their respective hemisphere (right and left), we are able to catagagorize and individual as "right-brained" or "left-brained" depending on what

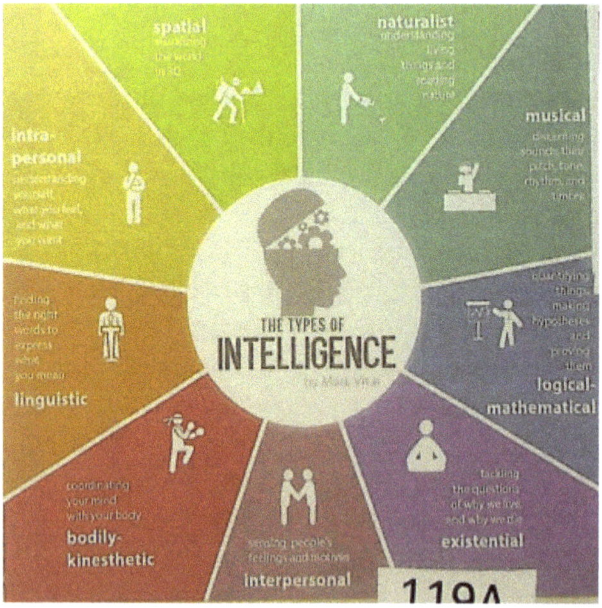

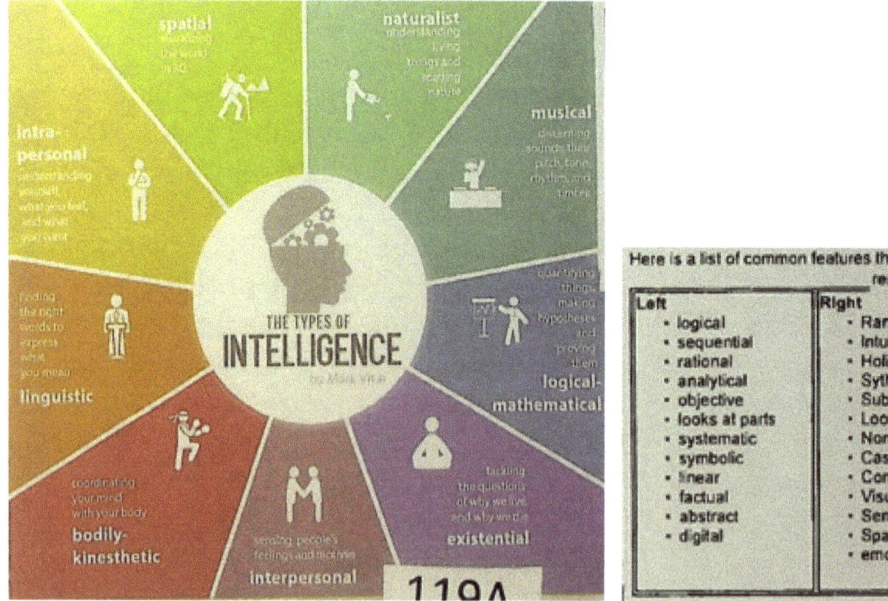

Here is a list of common features that show up on the respective naives:

Left	Right
• logical	• Random
• sequential	• Intuitive
• rational	• Holistic
• analytical	• Sythesizing
• objective	• Subjective
• looks at parts	• Looks at wholes
• systematic	• Non-verbal
• symbolic	• Casual
• linear	• Concrete
• factual	• Visual
• abstract	• Sensory
• digital	• Spatial
	• emotional

HYPOTHESIS #2

That the Failed group has been sufficiently restricted and restrained by the conventions, rules, laws, and mores by the dominant group that does not allow them the opportunely to learn, adapt and succeed.

Since 1865 legal slavery in the United States has been abolished, that's 152 years that has passed for some mitigation of the past pain and suffering of the Black slave descendants. Actually, none of the current descendants were slaves and have experienced zero physical pain to validate or justify the hell they are raising. Yes, of course I realize that we suffer the memory of our ancestor's agony, humiliation, oppression, and butchery; and the discrimination that has occurred BUT, WE haven't been raped, horse whipped, hung, sold to another person, or tarred and feathered...NO it was THEM, our great-great, great, and possibly grandparents who suffered. THEY deserve the apologies, the reparations, the good housing, the good jobs, the big new cars, the credit cards, etc; NOT us or YOU who may be reading this. WHY? BECAUSE they did the suffering. Now, I realize they are dead and cannot be made whole in any respect other than our love, reverence, memory and admiration for their strength, courage, discipline, faith and rugged perseverance to live and Survive that EVIL WHITE SLAVE OWNER and the Slave System: SO that you and I could be born and raised in a FREE SOCIETY as FREE men and women. They produced us in physical form (with GOD'S WILL), BUT their strength, courage, foresight, faith, LOVE and Smarts-intelligence has not survived them over these 152 years. We have become psychological slaves to the White man and don't even know it, flailing around, dancing, shucking and jiving, looking for a FREE anything, money without working, jobs without preparation, education without study, good health without bodily care, respect without earning it, LOVE when many of us HATE each other and Envy, Resent and Covet the success of our brethren and their material possessions. So, then we expect the White and Latino society to respect, love and pity us? PLEASE! Let's GET REAL - We must put on our "Big Boy Pants", so to speak, and make a life, and world for ourselves, like, the Jews, the Latinos and other immigrants who come to America with nothing, and in a few years, they are ahead of us, and we are buying our cigarettes, Red Bull, candy, fat-burgers, 40 ozs, cars, potato chips, furniture and various and sundry items FROM THEM. But NO, we cry discrimination, blame the White man, even the Boogie Man, any excuse for our FAILURE.

But before I go on, let's look at what the White man has actually done to help us, notwithstanding that he has done us wrong, and restrained our development in a racial-social sense in the past 152 years.

LEGISLATION, COURT DECISIONS, AND OTHER ACTIVITES RELEVANT TO OUR PROGRESS

1857 Dred Scott v Sanford (Denial of Basic Rights to Blacks) A major precursor to the Civil War, this controversial U.S. Supreme Court decision denied citizenship and basic rights to all Blacks - slave or free. (BAD)

1863 President Abraham Lincoln's "Emancipation Proclamation" takes effect proclaiming freedom from slavery for African Americans. (GOOD)

1865 The 13th Amendment to the U.S. Constitution is passed, abolishing slavery in the United States. (GOOD)

1868 The 14th Amendment to the U.S. Constitution is passed, guaranteeing due process and equal protection rights to all citizens. (GOOD)

1870 The 15th Amendment to the U.S. Constitution is passed, guaranteeing the right to vote for all U.S. citizens. (GOOD)

1896 Plessey v Ferguson (Approval of "separate but equal" Facilities. The U.S. Supreme Court approved laws requiring racial segregation, as long as those laws did not allow for separate accommodations and facilities for Blacks that were not inferior to those of Whites. (BAD)

1909 National Association for the Advancement of Colored People (NAACP) was Founded. (GOOD)

920 The 19th Amendment to the U.S. Constitution is passed, granting women the right to vote. (GOOD)

1954 Brown v Board of Education of Topeka, Kansas, Desegregation in Education Decision by the U.S, Supreme Court, abolishing the "separate but equal" law in education based on the 1896 Plessey v Ferguson decision. (Good)

1964 Civil Rights Act of 1964. Prohibits discrimination in a number of settings: voting, public accommodations, public facilities, public education and public assisted programs. (Good)

1965 Voting Rights Act of 1965 prohibits the denial or restriction of the right to Vote and forbids discriminatory practices nationwide. (GOOD).

1967 Loving v Virginia (Inter-racial Marriage), U.S. Supreme Court declares that laws prohibiting inter-racial marriage are unconstitutional. (GOOD)

1990 Americans with Disabilities Act. Protects people with disabilities from discrimination in many aspects of life, including employment, education, and access to public accommodations. (GOOD)

2015 Obergefell v Hodges (Rights of Same-sex Couples) U.S. Supreme Court decision declares same- sex marriage legal in all 50 states. 1948 Executive Order 9981, Issued by President Harry S. Truman desegregated the U.S armed forces. (GOOD)

1962 Executive Order 11063, Issued by President John F. Kennedy, banned segregation in federally funded housing. (GOOD).

1946 National School Lunch Act provided free and low-cost meals to qualified low-income students- on the idea that a "full stomach " supported class attendance and learning. (GOOD). This of course helped many poor Blacks as well as Whites.

I could continue with listing court decisions and legislation ad infinitim, that would support my thesis that there has been a continuous effort by the white majority to mitigate the painful experience and crippling effects of slavery, while acknowledging the fact that this effort has been limited and restricted by racist and discriminatory actions of some of that majority. YES, racism and discrimination are with us and will probably be with us, in the U.S. as well as in the whole world forever, so we MUST deal with it and DEFEAT it where we can, but NOT YIELD to it and cry and hide behind excuses for OUR FAILURE by riding the SLAVERY HORSE. It is TIRED and needs to be put out to Pasture so that it can die a peaceful DEATH. We MUST change our attitude, strategy, and tactics to defeat our problems and enemies, without violence, and without KILLING each other, or our situation will be MOOT, since we would have exterminated our OWN race by our OWN Hand. So, at the risk of not producing more examples of healing legislation and decisions, and to the benefit of saving some trees: I conclude that though acknowledging SOME restrictions to our progress, it has NOT been of sufficient quantity and intensity to qualify as the Major factor, that explains our demise and FAILURE to successfully navigate and assimilate this Euro-American culture of the United States. I must therefore conclude by default to the remaining hypothesis, that Hypothesis #2 FAILS and must also be REJECTED. However, before we address the final hypothesis, I wish to be CLEAR to the reader that I have "No Dog in This Fight" so to speak and take no pleasure in writing about this topic and revealing truths to those not aware or unfamiliar with such information. But to heal an Illness we must first acknowledge that we are Sick. And finally, I am NOT painting All Negro Black Americans as being irresponsible, unreliable, helpless, undisciplined and low in emotional intelligence and deductive reasoning that has led us to this BAD situation; But I AM including the 70% or so of us who DO fit this characterization. "SO IF THE SHOE DOESN'T FIT" please disregard because this is NOT personal.

HYPOTHESIS #3

That the Individual Behavior of the group is anti-social, criminal, and anti-ethical to the folkways, conventions, mores, and laws of the particular society.

My major proposition to support this hypothesis is that the African American Black male - according to the U.S. Census Bureau- is 21.5 million or 6.6% of the total United States population and 48% of the 43 million Blacks in America, with the other 52% being female. Of the 2.2 million persons in the U.S. jails, state, and federal prisons, 43% or 946,000 are Black males, U.S. Sentencing Project (2017). That is 43% of those incarcerated but only 6.6% of the population. That's over 600% higher representation in prison than their proportional representation in the entire country. In addition, according to Black Demographics, (2013), 34% of all working age (18-64 yrs.), Black men who are not incarcerated are ex-offenders, compared to 12% of all men, which means that at one point in their lives have been convicted of a felony. In employment, Black males age (16-64), had only a 67% labor force participation rate compared to the 80% for "all males"(IBID). In this same age group, 40% of Black males had NO earnings for 2013, (IBID). Finally, in Education in 2013, Black men had a bachelor's degree at 17% compared to 30% for "all men", (IBID).

Given just these data it appears, that Black men, especially YOUNG Black men are a drag on the success or progress to the Black race. The "tail wagging the dog" so to speak, even before we talk about violence and MURDER per se. My point here even before further analysis is that it is our BEHAVIOR that is destroying our race, NOT the COPS, NOT the KKK, NOT the WHITE SUPREMICISTS, NOT the BOOGIE MAN, NOT Discrimination, NO, IT IS US. WE are the ENEMY.

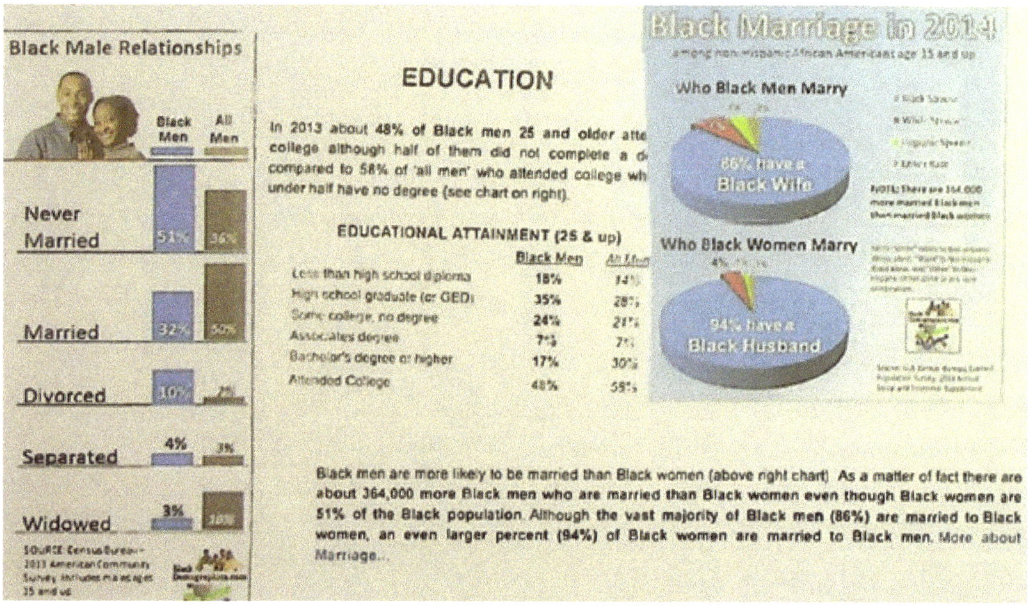

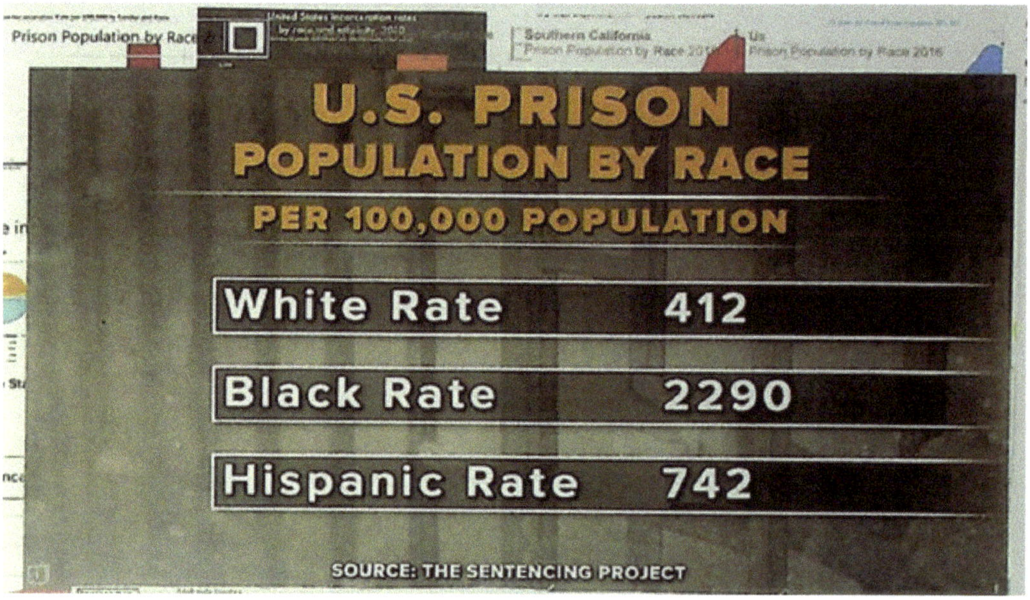

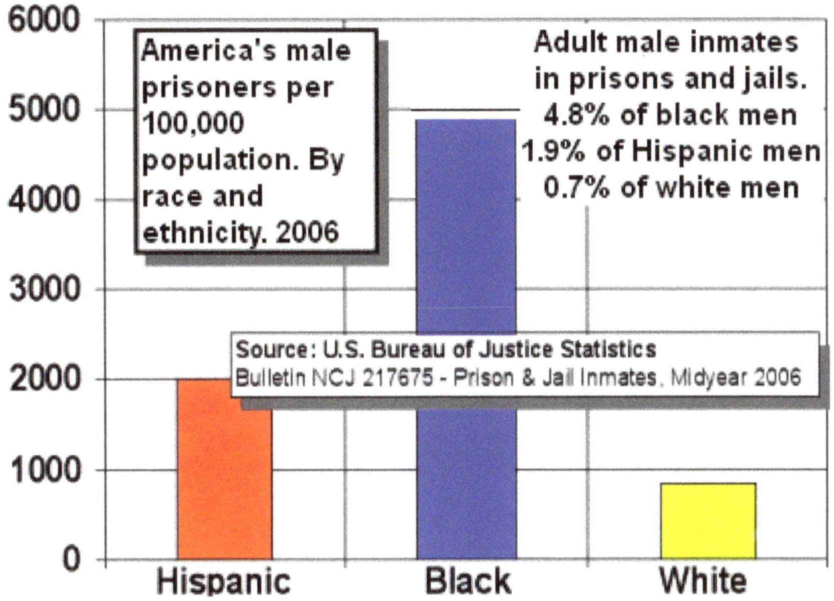

Percentages of black and white men exclude Hispanic men.

REGIONAL MURDER RATES, 2001 - 2015

MURDER RATES PER 100,000 PEOPLE

REGION	2015	2014	2013	2012	2011	2010	2009	2008	2007	2006	2005	2004	2003	2002	2001	EXECUTIONS SINCE 1976 (As of 03/15/17)
South	5.9	6.5	5.3	5.5	5.5	5.6	6.1	6.6	7.0	6.8	6.6	6.6	6.9	6.8	6.7	1180
Midwest	5.0	4.3	4.5	4.7	4.5	4.4	4.6	4.8	4.9	5.0	4.9	4.7	4.9	5.1	5.3	180
West	4.2	3.9	4.0	4.2	4.2	4.2	4.6	5.0	5.3	5.6	5.8	5.7	5.7	5.7	5.5	85
Northeast	3.5	3.3	3.5	3.8	3.9	4.2	3.8	4.2	4.1	4.5	4.4	4.2	4.2	4.1	4.2	4
NATIONAL RATE	4.9	4.5	4.5	4.7	4.7	4.8	5.0	5.4	5.6	5.7	5.6	5.5	5.7	5.6	5.6	

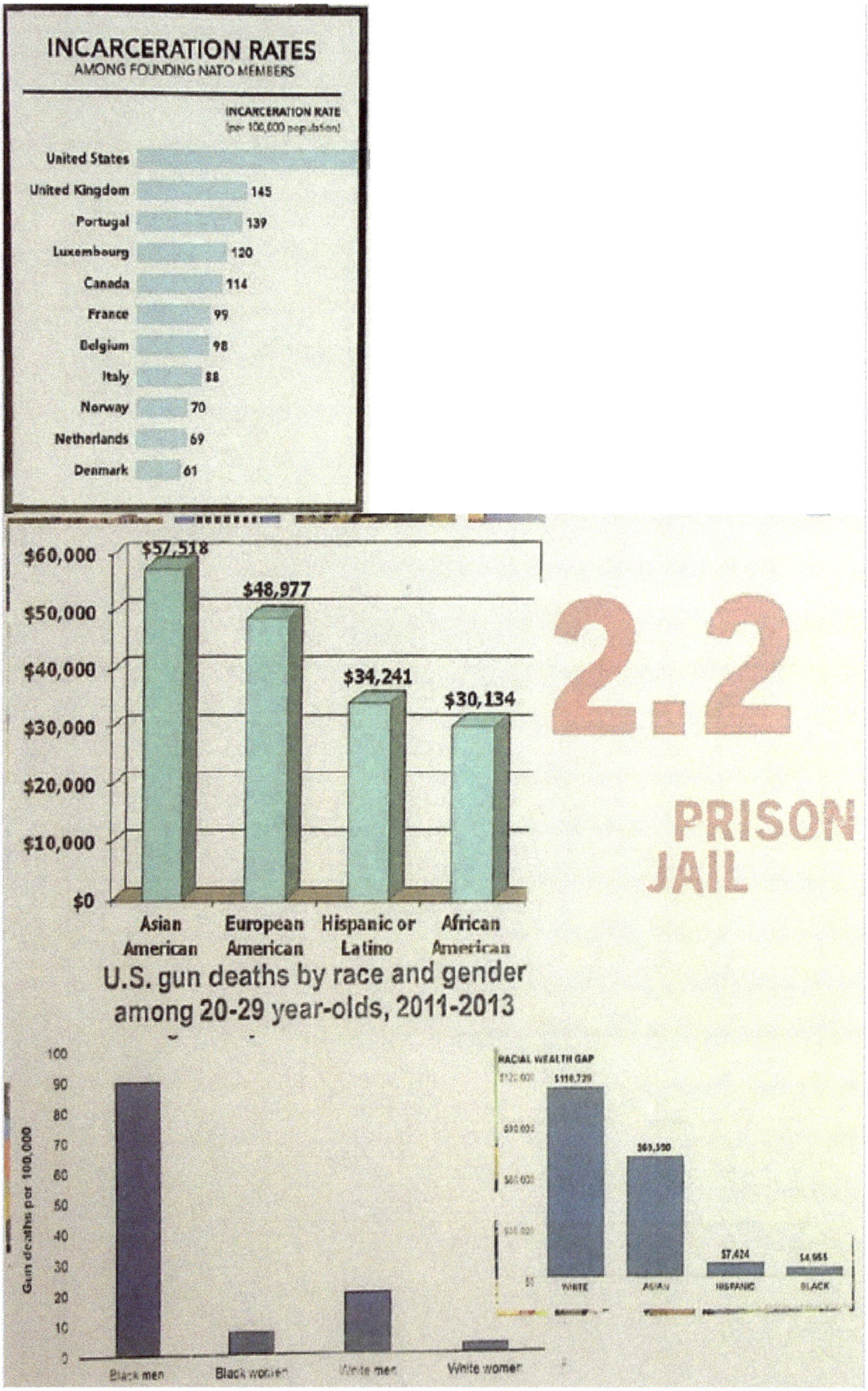
INCARCERATION RATES
AMONG FOUNDING NATO MEMBERS
INCARCERATION RATE
United States
United Kingdom 145
Portugal 139
Luxembourg 120
Canada 114
France 99
Belgium 98
Italy 88
Norway 70
Netherlands 69
Denmark 61
$60,000
$50,000
$40,000
$30,000
$20,000
$10,000
$0
$48,977
$34,241
$30,134
Asian American
European American
Hispanic or Latino
African American
2.2
PRISON
JAIL
U.S. gun deaths by race and gender
among 20-29 year-olds, 2011-2013
Gun deaths per 100,000
100
90
80
70
60
50
40
30
20
10
0
Black men
Black women
White women
$7,424
WHITE
BLACK

https://www.leg.state.nv.us/Session/79th2017/Exhibits/Assembly/JUD/AJUD526E.pdf.

So, what is it that is pushing us, influencing us to be violent, undisciplined, dangerous, unreliable, deceptive, and anti-social to put us at the bottom of society? I will now advance the proposition of applying Sociological, Criminology- Strain Theory to this dilemma.

SOCIAL STRAIN THEORY

Social Strain Theory was developed in 1938 by Robert K. Merton, Merton, Robert (1938). "Social Structure and Anomie". American Sociological Review, 3 (5): 62-682. The theory states that society puts pressure on individuals to achieve socially accepted goals (such as the American dream) though they lack the means, this leads to strain which may lead the individual to commit crimes. Examples being selling drugs or becoming involved in prostitution to gain financial security, (IBID). Merton continued on to say that, when faced with strain, people have five ways to adapt, (IBID).

1. Conformity: pursuing cultural goals through socially approved means. "Hopeful Poor".

2. Innovation: using socially unapproved or unconventional means to obtain culturally approved goals.

Such as dealing drugs or stealing to achieve financial security. "Surviving Poor".

3. 3. Ritualism: using the same socially approved means to achieve less elusive goals, more modest and humbler. ("Passive Poor").

4. Retreatism: to reject both the cultural goals and the means to obtain it, then find a way to escape it. "Retreating Poor".

5. Rebellion: to reject the goals and means, then work to replace them. "Resisting Poor".

Strain Theory is not without its critics. (1) is that it best applies only to the lower class as they struggle with limited resources to obtain their goals, (2) that it fails to explain white collar crime, and (3) it fails to explain crimes based on gender inequality. This criticism is fine with me since I am only concerned with the struggle of essentially lower-class Blacks in this treatise.

Crime, Malefactors, and the Criminal Industrial Complex

According to the Sentencing Project, (2017), a Washington , D.C. based group that advocates for prison reform, one in every three Black males born today (2017), can expect to go to prison at some point in their life, compared to one in every six Latinos, and one in every seventeen white males, if current incarceration trends continue; and records show that today Black males makeup 43% or 986,000 of the 2.3 million prisoners incarcerated in local, state and federal jails and prisons in the United States-today. Yet the Black male is only 6.6% of the population of the United States.

This is grossly out of a normal distributional proportion to what would be expected for a population of their size. WHY IS THIS SO? The CBS Philly report (2014) indicates that 49% of Black males are arrested NOW before their 23rd birthday. WHY? But wait! It gets worse. According to Victor Thorne, (2014), 53% of Black males and 38% of whites will be arrested by their 23rd year by 2017 at the current rates. Aaron Bandler, (2016) in his research on Black crime found that 93% of Black murders are committed by other Blacks. He continues that from 1980-2008,52% of ALL American murders were committed by Blacks even though they are only 13% of the population. So, this begs the question of WHY are the Young Black males so violent and criminal MALEFACTORS? Some say it is the reaction and rebellion to White racism and discrimination. Others say it is the result of poverty-lending credibility to the Strain Theory, but many, many countries in the world are much poorer than the American Black, yet their criminality and crime rate is much less. Our crime and murder rate are among the highest in the world even though most Black as well as White poor have at least one color TV, a beat up car, air condition, heat, food stamps, EBT (electronic benefit transfer card) subsidized (free) health care, subsidized housing (section 8), low priced and free school lunches, meals on wheels and so on, YET, we still steal, rob, game the system, cheat, lie about income, don't pay any taxes except sales tax, and RAPE and Murder. What is wrong with US, are we just natural predators and beggars always looking for something FREE, and no matter how much we receive even though many don't work, or wouldn't work in a PIE Factory, we are never satisfied, and cry for MORE FREEBIES. And the worst of the Madness, is that when given the opportunity to escape the "oppressed environment of ghetto poverty" we escape FROM potential FREEDOM and remain in our ostensible " cocoon of comfort" "GO FIGURE".

Witten, Colonel V. (2017) Black Escape from Freedom: The Fallacy of Victimism, and the Resulting Self-Defeating Behavior and Avoidance of Responsibility.

Dr Thomas Sowell, (2015) the famous Black philosopher, psychiatrist and syndicated columnist observes that in the 1940s and 1950s, Black poverty and racism was higher than it is today, But the crime rate was much lower. He continues that before 1960 most Black children lived in two parent families and had appropriate structure, order, and discipline. He has observed that in 2013, 72% of Blacks were born out of wedlock. Sowell concludes that the primary culprit is the breakdown of the Black two parent nuclear family. Only 15% of white children were born out of wedlock. This concept of the family being the first agent of socialization is a bedrock principle in Sociology, where the child learns and internalizes attitudes, values, beliefs, behaviors, role models and identifications. Children in "broken" homes" as a result tend to suffer from a range of problems. Problems such as low self-esteem and emotional instability. According to Alan Schwartz, growing up without a father has a profound effect on boys that last into manhood. Boys need a father to learn how to become a man. They tend to grow up undisciplined and are likely to experience depression and anxiety, Schwartz, A. (2009). With 73% of Black boys and girls born into fatherless homes, it is no wonder that they are out of control and antisocial.

Emotional Intelligence

Another important factor to consider as we move closer to the end of this inquiry and assessment of our dilemma is our Emotional Intelligence (El). Emotional intelligence is the capability of individuals to recognize their own and other people's emotions, discern between different feelings and label them appropriately, use emotional information to guide thinking and behavior, and manage and/or adjust emotions to adapt to environments or achieve one's goal(s). Coleman, Andrew (2008), A Dictionary of Psychology (3rd) Oxford University Press.

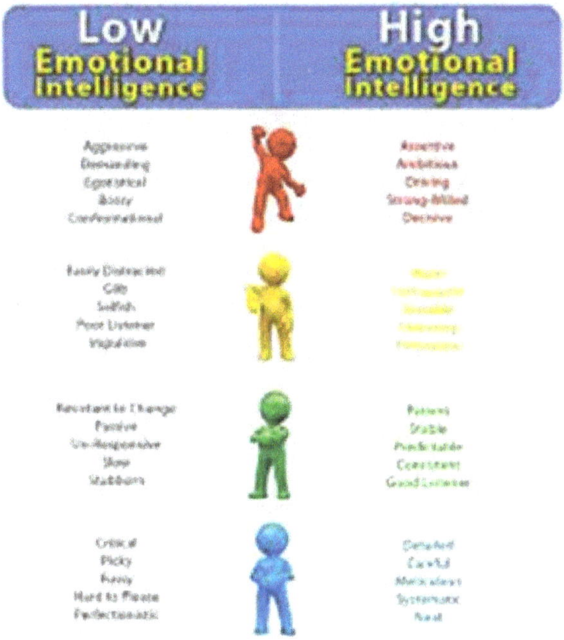

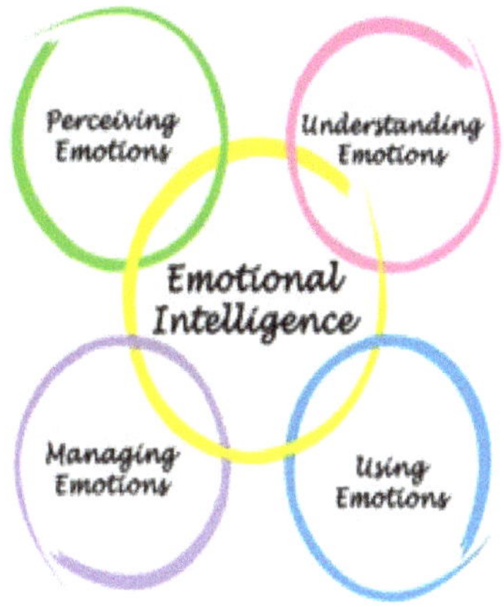

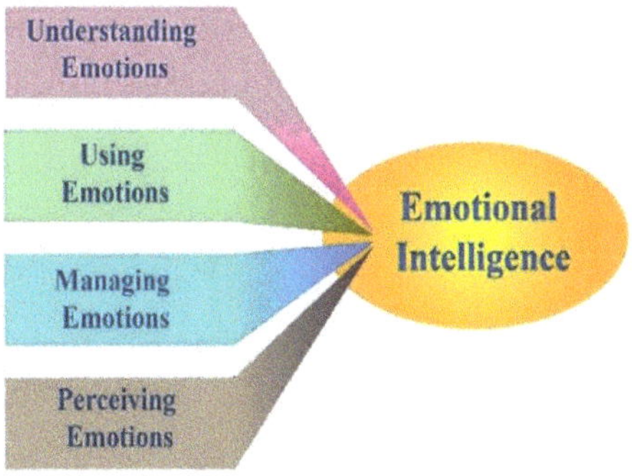

Tavis Smiley, a Black talk show host and liberal political activist says Black people are too emotional to obey rules,(June 2007, C-Span) Tons of psychological studies have resulted in outcomes that show that Black people have low El -Emotional intelligence- i.e.; lacks or has low ability to delay gratification, difficulty understanding the concept of responsibility, have poor self-regulation, low empathy, weak self-awareness and have difficulty controlling their emotions, Goldman, (1995), Whitman et al, Wiley Online, April 2014. Richard Lynn, (2002) advances the theory that these are factors that account for Black high crime rates. Deborrah Cooper, (2010) while discussing the emotionally abusive Black man, postulates that both depression and obesity are at epidemic levels amongst Black women in the United States and believe these afflictions are attributable to stressful interactions and relationships with Black men. She continues with the hypothesis that most abusive Black men tend to be those that feel most powerless, least confident, and most insecure about their abilities and accomplishments, (IBID).

These men in the U.S., mostly Black, in familial, romantic, or social environments tend to demonstrate a marked disdain and lack of respect for Black women. She contends that Black men present themselves as toxic, full of rage and project this insecurity and fear onto Black women at every opportunity. Whether in public and or among strangers or romantic relationships, their communications with Black women are laden with critical behavior, (IBID).

It's important to impress their buddies and prove they are a man by shaming women. Deborrah (2010) asserts that Black men never apologize because what they do is done on purpose to break the woman's spirit and gain power over her. He is initially nice to her and makes her happy, then pulls the rug out and watches her crash. Feeling confused and wounded, the woman feels guilty that she did something to make him "change" and accepts the shift in blame, and now he has control over her happiness, Deborrah, (IBID).

We now move to the general effect of how this 70% is influenced and manipulated by the social media, emotional effect of past slavery, loss of self-esteem and the take "no prisoners" in the zero-sum game of capitalism.

IF

-RVDYARD KIPLING

IF YOU CAN KEEP YOUR HEAD WHEN ALL ABOUT YOU
ARE LOSING THEIRS AND BLAMING IT ON YOU;
IF YOU CAN TRUST YOURSELF WHEN ALL MEN DOUBT YOU;
BUT MAKE ALLOWANCE FOR THEIR DOUBTING TOO,
IF YOU CAN WAIT AND NOT BE TIRED BY WAITING,
OR, BEING LIED ABOUT DON'T DEAL IN LIES,
OR, BEING HATED, DON'T GIVE WAY TO HATING,
AND YET DON'T LOOK TOO GOOD, NOR TALK TOO WISE;
IF YOU CAN DREAM-AND NOT MAKE DREAMS YOUR MASTER
IF YOU CAN THINK-AND NOT MAKE THOUGHTS YOUR AIM;
IF YOU CAN MEET WITH TRIUMPH AND DISASTER
AND TREAT THOSE TWO IMPOSTORS JUST THE SAME,
IF YOU CAN BEAR TO HEAR THE TRUTH YOU'VE SPOKEN .
TWISTED BY KNAVES TO MAKE A TRAP FOR FOOLS,
OR WATCH THE THINGS YOU GAVE YOUR LIFE TO BROKEN,
AND STOOP AND BUILD 'EM UP WITH WORN OUT TOOLS;
IF YOU CAN MAKE ONE HEAP OF ALL YOUR WINNINGS
AND RISK IT ON ONE TURN OF PITCH-AND -TOSS,
AND LOSE, AND START AGAIN AT YOUR BEGINNINGS
AND NEVER BREATHE A WORD ABOUT YOUR LOSS;
IF YOU CAN FORCE YOUR HEART ND NERVE AND SINEW
TO SERVE YOUR TURN LONG AFTER THEY ARE GONE,
AND SO BOLD ON WHEN THERE IS NOTHING IN YOU
EXCEPT THE WILL WHICH SAYS TO THEM:"HOLD ON";
IF YOU CAN TALK WITH CROWDS AND KEEP YOUR VIRTUE,
OR WALK WITH KINGS-NOR LOSE THE COMMON TOUCH;
IF NEITHER FOES NOR LOVING FRIENDS CAN HURT YOU;
IF ALL MEN COUNT WITH YOU, BUT NONE TOO MUCH;
IF YOU CAN FILL THE UNFORGIVING MINUTE
WITH SIXTY SECONDS' WORTH OF DISTANCE RUN
' YOURS IS THE EARTH AND EVERYTHING THAT'S IN IT,
AND-WHICH IS MORE YOU'LL BE A MAN, MY SON!

Chapter Ten

Low Hanging Fruit

The concept or euphemism of the term "Low Hanging Fruit" is based on the notion of being "easy" to take or to influence or predict. The lower the apples are to the ground, the easier they are to pick, so to speak. The metaphor of doing the simplest or easiest work first, for the quick fix that produces ripe delectable results, or that the target to influence is easy to sell, fits many Black Americans spot on.

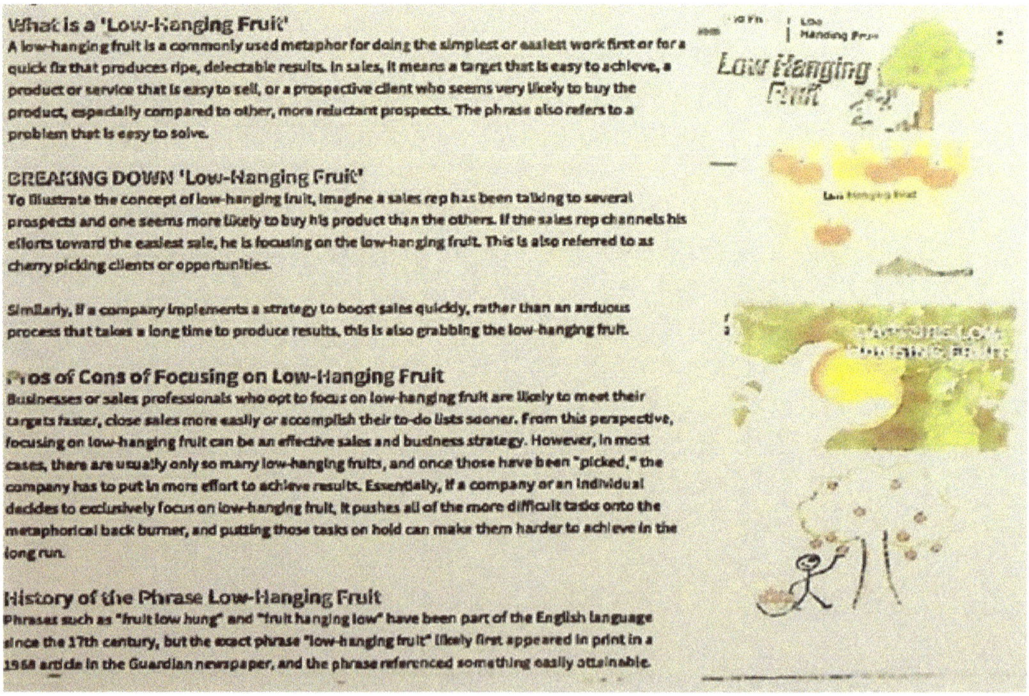

What is a 'Low-Hanging Fruit'

A low-hanging fruit is a commonly used metaphor for doing the simplest or easiest work first or for a quick fix that produces ripe, delectable results. In sales, it means a target that is easy to achieve, a product or service that is easy to sell, or a prospective client who seems very likely to buy the product, especially compared to other, more reluctant prospects. The phrase also refers to a problem that is easy to solve.

BREAKING DOWN 'Low-Hanging Fruit'

To illustrate the concept of low-hanging fruit, imagine a sales rep has been talking to several prospects and one seems more likely to buy his product than the others. If the sales rep channels his efforts toward the easiest sale, he is focusing on the low-hanging fruit. This is also referred to as cherry picking clients or opportunities.

Similarly, if a company implements a strategy to boost sales quickly, rather than an arduous process that takes a long time to produce results, this is also grabbing the low-hanging fruit.

Pros of Cons of Focusing on Low-Hanging Fruit

Businesses or sales professionals who opt to focus on low-hanging fruit are likely to meet their targets faster, close sales more easily or accomplish their to-do lists sooner. From this perspective, focusing on low-hanging fruit can be an effective sales and business strategy. However, in most cases, there are usually only so many low-hanging fruits, and once those have been "picked," the company has to put in more effort to achieve results. Essentially, if a company or an individual decides to exclusively focus on low-hanging fruit, it pushes all of the more difficult tasks onto the metaphorical back burner, and putting those tasks on hold can make them harder to achieve in the long run.

History of the Phrase Low-Hanging Fruit

Phrases such as "fruit low hung" and "fruit hanging low" have been part of the English language since the 17th century, but the exact phrase "low-hanging fruit" likely first appeared in print in a 1968 article in the Guardian newspaper, and the phrase referenced something easily attainable.

What do I mean by the statement that Blacks are low hanging fruit in America that benefits others but not the Blacks themselves? That we are easy pickings for our capitalist system to manage and dominate. Yes, we complain, cry discrimination, rob, kill each other-and occasionally a white person, vote in small numbers, cost the government lots of welfare money and produce lots of criminals for the prison industry. BUT it is effectively a small price for the power structure to pay-to Remain in Power. We now look at some categories in which it is Illustrated that this is so.

1 POLITICS/VOTING: We can be counted on to vote around 90% or more for Democrats in most any election, 99% if the candidate is Black. We vote with our heart-Not our head. Everything is emotional. We are attracted to the form and appearance of things, not it's substance. We are easily conned into doing things against our own self-interest without inquiry or scrutiny because the speaker or politician is "cool" or polished, or Black, with no concern for their qualifications or the long-term results of the proposals and the reality of the promises being fulfilled. If it is quick, easy and Free, we jump at it, often to our peril. And when they lie to us, we continue to vote for them next time. They don't have to spend much money on us because they already have us in their pocket. So, the politicians concentrate on the Hispanics and Whites who are higher up in the tree and harder to pick.

2 EDUCATION: We are easy here also. Our children receive an 8th grade education when receiving a high school diploma. But we are happy and proud and celebrate. Yes, we should be proud but not happy because we have been duped that our child has a REAL high school education. That piece of paper is practically worthless, most students can't get into a top college and if they do about 75% flunk out or drop out. Most cannot effectively read, write, cipher, or infer knowledge or information. They can barely do the work in HBCUs, and barely graduate in most cases with a "C" average, that's worth a good high school education. As long as we continue to allow the school systems to under educate our children right under our nose, we will continue to be "EASY" to dominate in every field of our society, while we are dancing, gambling and squandering our EBT from the SNAP program. So as long as we are content with the way it is without demanding change, the system will never take us seriously.

3 AUTOMOBILES: Cars/Trucks- We like pretty flashy, shiny things, often even when they don't work, are expensive and perishable. You see in many cases we have such low self-esteem, that we have to identify with something else that is valuable, recognized, worthy, or loved which will make us valuable and worthy. To a large degree many of us have been robbed of our intrinsic value, self-esteem and pride; so we get it through artificial and materialistic means, like big pretty cars, jewelry, big houses and for our men - a White woman. So, what do we do if and when we hit the numbers, win the lottery, win an accident case or otherwise come into a large sum of money, we run right out and buy a Cadillac, Mercedes, Lincoln or a $70,000 Pickup truck. NOW we are SOMEBODY and can show it off. Now we can be "seen", recognized, and given some attention which is what we lacked in the first place. Of course, the car dealerships love us as we continue on our "bridge to nowhere".

4 WELFARE AND POVERTY: We are EASY PIKENS to continue to participate in the Welfare Industrial complex. Without us millions of welfare workers and politicians would be out of a job. You see, in this context we are important and valuable for we keep them employed. They know that we will always be there for them, as cannon fodder for "their check". And for that We get a check, EBT card, subsidized housing and other elements of the SNAP program. Yes, of course we get a benefit of daily subsistence survival, but that is as far as most will go as long as we are content to stay at this level. But the soothing effect of a guaranteed check every month is too powerful a "koolaid", to risk giving up and work our way out of this quasi slavery. To escape this situation is fearful, for one would have to trade a guaranteed survival of a Big Fish in a small pond with the risk of being a small fish in a BIG OCEAN.

5 Disease, Unhealthy Diet and Death.
We are Easy pickings for cancer, heart disease, diabetes kidney/dialysis, high cholesterol, drug addiction and AIDS. We love our fat back, pork chops, pig feet, hog maws, alcohol, sugary drinks and other killer forms of fast food and drinks. OH, I forgot chitterlins. Yes, I know much of the preference for these fatty, sodium filled foods have been modeled and passed down to us from slavery traditions, but we now know the danger of these foods that causes most of the diseases we incur, yet we still eat them. The Black male especially-with a life expectancy 5 to 7 years less than a White man and even less for the White woman or Black woman; is most at risk.

Though unhealthy foods are a major component in our early death, murder-homicide is the primary killer of the young Black male 95% by other Black males, with an occasional killing by police-some perpetrated as suicide by cop. One study I recall-absent of reference- revealed that once a Black man makes it to 65, he has a better chance of living to be 95 than the average White man.

6 GAMBLING: We just love to gamble and are suckers in our effort to get something easy or free. It usually backfires and we lose more than we win-but we keep doing it. The gambling casinos, lotteries and the "numbers" are made to order for us. Many can't resist gambling the rent money or car payment on some get rich scheme or fancy advertisement that ends up taking our money. And of course, we love to buy the scratch off at the gas station. There are so many in line that it is difficult to just buy gas. We are easy pigeons for the deceptive and crippling lies we are told about our chances to win, AND EVEN when we are told the odds are 10,000,000 to 1, we still plunk down our $2. And don't even go to a 'Tree" cookout. The people will be lined up coming out of the "woodwork" to get the free food, and then add insult to injury by taking one or two "plates" home with them.

I could go on, but I think this enough. The factors of poverty, discrimination, crime, religion, slavery, health, cognitive style, culture, fear of failure, education and psychology have been addressed in this treatise and examined for relevant strength and influence on our behavior. I admit I have not teased out or discovered the "smoking gun" that has placed us here, BUT we are HERE, and it is REAL. We are on a slippery slope to DOOM and ignore it at our PERIL. The ball is in the readers court and requires some introspection if interested. I am only the MESSENGER.

Colonel Vaughan Witten, PhD.

ADDENDUM

>Abraham Lincoln Leadership Principles
>Old Wine in New Bottles
>List to Live By Conservative Black Leaders
>Warning to Black America
>Johnson-Casor Slave Trial Transcript
>U.S. Slave Map in 1861 Clack Slang Glossary
>Drawing of idealized slavery life as depicted by slave-owners view
>Images of Black and Indian Slave owners

PRINCIPLES OF LEADERSHIP BY ABRAHAM LINCOLN

Abraham Lincoln overcame the almost insurmountable problems of holding a nation together that was torn by civil war and divided on the issue of slavery. He was able to win the war, free the slaves and preserve the nation as a whole body under a constitution as amended; grounded on the principles of liberty, justice, freedom and the pursuit of happiness. His strong leadership in this endeavor was supported by the following leadership principles which can be applied to corporations and educational institutions today.

I. It is important that people know you come among them without fear.
II. Seek casual contact with your subordinates. It is as meaningful as a formal gathering, if not more so.
III. Remember, everyone likes a compliment.
IV. You must seek and require access to reliable and up-to-date information.
V. Give your subordinates a fair chance with equal freedom and opportunity for success.
VI. Wage only one war at a time and choose your battles.
VII. When you extinguish hope, you create desperation.
VIII. Never crush a man out, thereby making him and his friends, permanent enemies of your organization.
IX. Remember: your organization will take on the personality of its top leader.
X. Make no explanation to your enemies. What they want is a squabble and fuss; and that they can have if you explain, and they cannot have if you don't.
XI. Try not to feel insecure or threatened by your followers.
XII. Always let your subordinates know that the honor will be theirs if they succeed and the blame will be yours if they fail.
XIII. Surround yourself with people who really know their business, and avoid "yes" men.
XIV. Remember that the best leaders never stop learning.

Compiled and edited by,
Vaughan Witten, Ph.D Psychologist
Vice President for Student Affairs Shaw University and
Chief Master Sergeant USAF (RET)

A List to Live By

The most destructive habit	WORRY
The greatest joy	GIVING
The greatest loss	SELF-RESPECT
The most endangered species	DEDICATED LEADERS
The most satisfying work	HELPING OTHERS
The ugliest personality trait	SELFISHNESS
Our greatest natural resource	OUR YOUTH
The greatest "shot in the arm"	ENCOURAGEMENT
The greatest problem to overcome	FEAR
The most effective sleeping pill	PEACE OF MIND
The most powerful force in life	LOVE
The most crippling failure disease	EXCUSES
The most dangerous pariah	A GOSSIPER
The world's most incredible computer	THE BRAIN
The worst thing to be without	HOPE
The deadliest weapon	THE TONGUE
The most power-filled words	"I CAN"
The greatest asset	FAITH
The most worthless emotion	SELF-PITY
The most beautiful attire	A SMILE
The most prized possession	INTEGRITY
The most powerful channel of Communication	PRAYER
The most contagious spirit	ENTHUSIAM

For a Long Healthy, Wealthy, Wise Life, My Advice

° Love God, parents, and family
° Love America and fight for her when necessary
• Don't smoke, do drugs, or drink excessively
° Don't covet or envy
° Don't run red lights
° Don't mess with another person's wife or husband
• Read good books and all newspapers

• Eat breakfast
• Work hard and work smart
° Save some money
• Don't Ioan money to friends or anyone - It only makes enemies
* Get education - write a book and plant a tree
s Don't gossip ‘
° Obey the law
Everyone needs this list to live by... then everyone can really be successful!

FAMOUS BLACK AMERICAN CONSERVATIVES

Idiot Black Politicians and Race Hustlers: Van Jones, Cory Booker, Maxine Waters, Al Sharpton

Advice and warning for African-Americans/Blacks

(For those who this shoe fits)

Throw away the cell phones and "bling-bling". 2. Get out of bed and report on time. Read, read, read — books, newspapers, anything. 3. Take personal responsibility and stop blaming? Others for your inadequacies, flaws, poverty. 4. Be proud of yourself and don't depend on others for your self-worth, self-esteem, and value. 5. Work hard, respect self and others. Be truthful, honest and get it done-no excuses-no complaints. Otherwise, you will continue to be treated and perceived as second, third class, and the Whites, Chinese, Indians, Hispanics will disregard and destroy you as irrelevant and unworthy of a seat at the table. The old saying about Blacks: "If you want to keep a secret from them - Write It Down."

I am continuing this section in the reprint - not in the original manuscript. I am somewhat reluctant to say this, but if only one person understands or agrees, then it is worth it. So here goes. Many but not all of us Blacks enjoy our victimization status. This is primarily young Blacks who have been conditioned by the Government to be dependent on it for survival, primarily to get us to love it, support it and keep them, primarily Democrats in power. So, the more food stamps we get- even if we don't quality, section 8 housing, anything free or purportedly free, we pursue. In effect we become defacto slaves to the Government and often refuse to move from our dependent comfort zone to one of independence and freedom. Hans Selye, the famous psychologist calls this learned helplessness. Now don't get mad. I'm not characterizing all Blacks this way. But a significant number - which does not include the proud hard-working people of West Virginia. Eric Fromm, another psychologist has a similar theory of Escape from Freedom. In other words, many Blacks and Whites prefer the comfort of protection and sympathy to the risk of being free and subject to the vagaries and problems of life that comes with true liberty and freedom. Yes, we have a class society of achievement, money, education, and sophisticated manners. Most of us love to work for these. But freedom is not free, and liberty must be a constant pursuit.

It is a pity that we -not all- have lost our Christian spirit and values we had when in physical bondage and turned Martin Luther King's philosophy on its head by now - judging people by the color of their skin instead of the content of their character. Many of us who have succumbed to the entitlement and welfare state would vote for a retarded criminal Black over a White Socrates, Lincoln, Truman and Descartes wrapped into one. Blacks and Whites of my generation will be ok, but the pampered, weak, delusional bunch that will soon control America - I can only see poverty, decay, subjugation and third world status for the future.

Finally, we have moved from responsibility, accountability, and obedience to God, to worship the golden calf, to the self-destruction of covet. From need to want, earn and pay to hook me up, to get over - defraud the system with no guilt and education without study. We want as much as we can get from others for free. We violate daily, the Thou shall Not Covet commandment of the Ten from Moses and God, much less the other 603 from Moses that most don't even know about. Our childish indulgence in outrageous liberty and behavior is chipping away at our basic freedom and will undo everything we have gained since 1865. Think about it. This is primarily directed to the 40 and under crowd.

Covet-To strongly want something another person has, to long for with envy-greedy. To want to possess another's money, goods, wife, husband, house and etc.

ENCYCLOPEDIA VIRGINIA

PRIMARY RESOURCE

Court Ruling on Anthony Johnson and His Servant (1655)
Transcription from Original

The deposition of Captain Samuel Goldsmith taken (in open court) 8th of March Sayth, That beinge at the howse of Anthony Johnson Negro (about the beginninge of November last to receive a hogshead of tobacco) a Negro called John Casar came to this Deponent, and told him that hee came into Virginia for seaven or Eight yeares (per Indenture) And that hee had demanded his freedome of his master Anthony Johnson; And further said that Johnson had kept him his servant seaven yeares longer than hee ought, And desired that this deponent would see that hee might have noe wronge, whereupon your Deponent demanded of Anthony Johnson his Indenture, hee answered, hee never sawe any; The said Negro (John Casor) replyed, hee came for a certayne tyme and had an Indenture Anthony Johnson said hee never did see any But that hee had him for his life; Further this deponent saith That mr. Robert Parker and George Parker they knew that the said Negro had an Indenture (in on Mr. Carye hundred on the other side of the Baye) And the said Anthony Johnson did not tell the negro goe free The said John Casor would recover most of his Cowes of him; Then Anthony Johnson (as this deponent did suppose) was in a feare. Upon this his Sonne in lawe, his wife and his 2 sonnes perswaded the said Anthony Johnson to sett the said John Casor free. more saith not

Samuel Goldsmith

This daye Anthony Johnson Negro made his complaint to the Court against mr. Robert Parker and declared that hee deteyneth his servant John Casor negro (under pretence that the said Negro is a free man.) The Court seriously consideringe and maturely weighinge the premisses, doe fynde that the said Mr. Robert Parker most unjustly keepeth the said Negro from Anthony Johnson his master as appeareth by the deposition of Captain Samuel Goldsmith and many probably circumstances. It is therefore the Judgment of the Court and ordered That the said John Casor Negro forthwith returne unto the service of his said master Anthony Johnson, And that mr. Robert Parker make payment of all charge in the suit. also Execution.

Author Transcription Source

Northhampton County Court Northampton County Order Book 1655-1668, fol. 10; via Warren M. Billings, ed., The Old Dominion in the Seventeenth Century: A Documentary History of Virginia, 1606-1689 (Chapel Hill: The University of North Carolina Press. 1975) P 180 181.

On March 8, 1655, the Northampton County Court ruled in favor of Anthony Johnson, a free man of African descent, when he was accused of keeping an indentured servant as a slave.

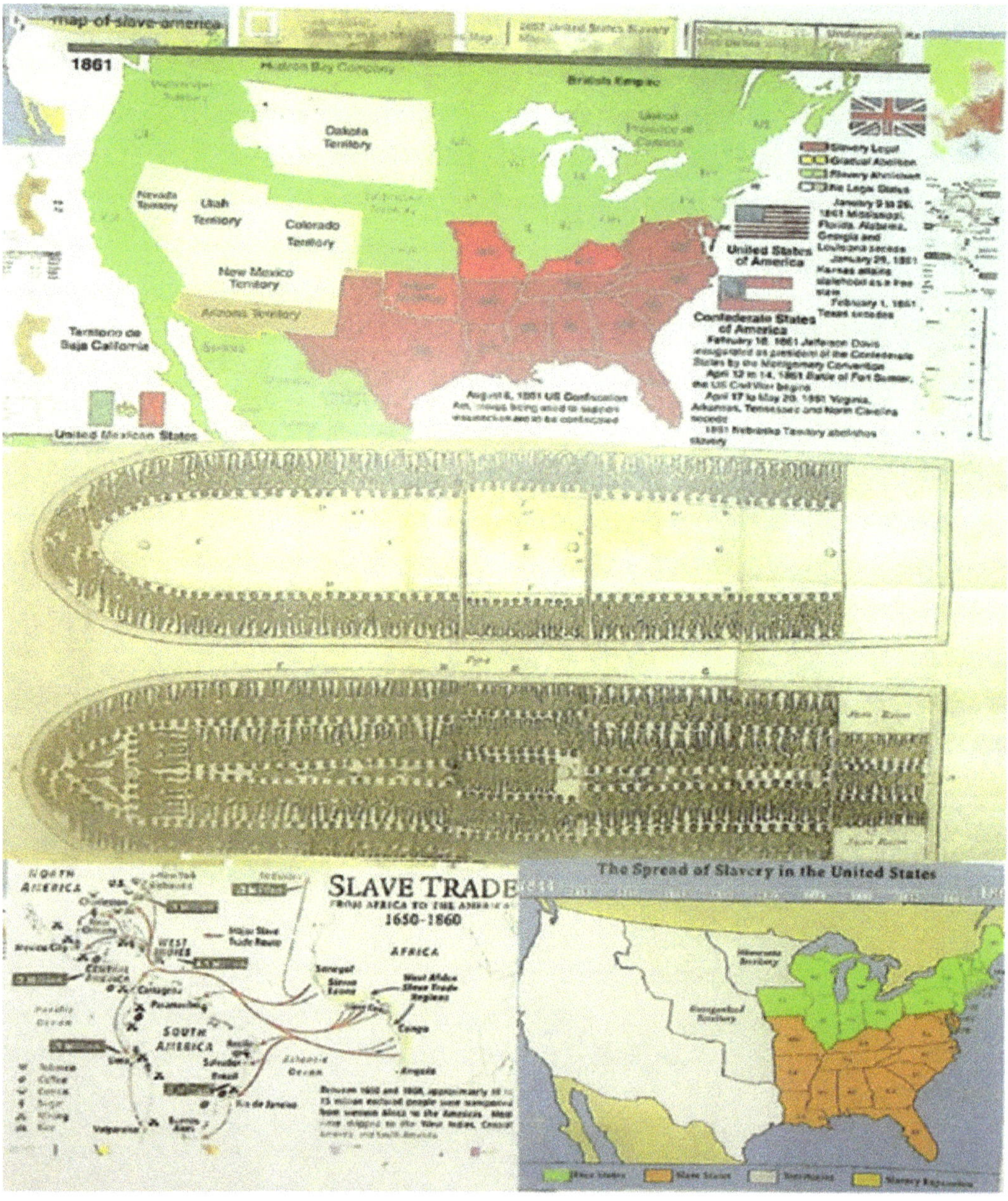

Glossary - Black Slang

AKA- Also known as
Apple- Indian, Red on outside and White on inside
Africant- Unemployed lazy Black
Benjamin- 100 dollar bills
Bear- Black, educated and rich
Biscuit lip- Large lips
Crime factory- Black women breeding future criminals
Crime stopper- Black woman having an abortion
Diesel- Muscular
DWB- Driving while black
EBT- Electronic Benefit Transfer card, aka Food stamp card
Ghost rider- Blacks having sex with whites
Going postal- Going crazy with anger- wild
Hambone- Overweight man
Horse- Heroin
Hillbilly heroin- Narcotic drug Oxycodone
Niglet- A young N-word person
Oreo- Black on out side and white on inside
Pineapple- Blacks who act like Asians
Popolo- Hiwaiian for "black person"
Red bone- Hi yellow, light skinned black
Rope head- Young black woman with braided weave hair
Salty- Angry over a minor issue or situation
Sneakers- Always come in pairs
Six- Good PC way to say nigger without getting jumped on. Can say "look at that 6 over there".
Tootsie roll- Black children
40- Forty oz of beer or some drink
925- LA Police code for suspicious person
Skag- Unattractive or promiscuous woman
Black gold- Oil
Word- "I understand you totally".
Swag- Looking sharp, awesome
Flexing- Showing off
YOLO- You only live once
Meltdown- Total collapse
Pig out- Binge eating
Ratchet- Ugly, nasty appearance

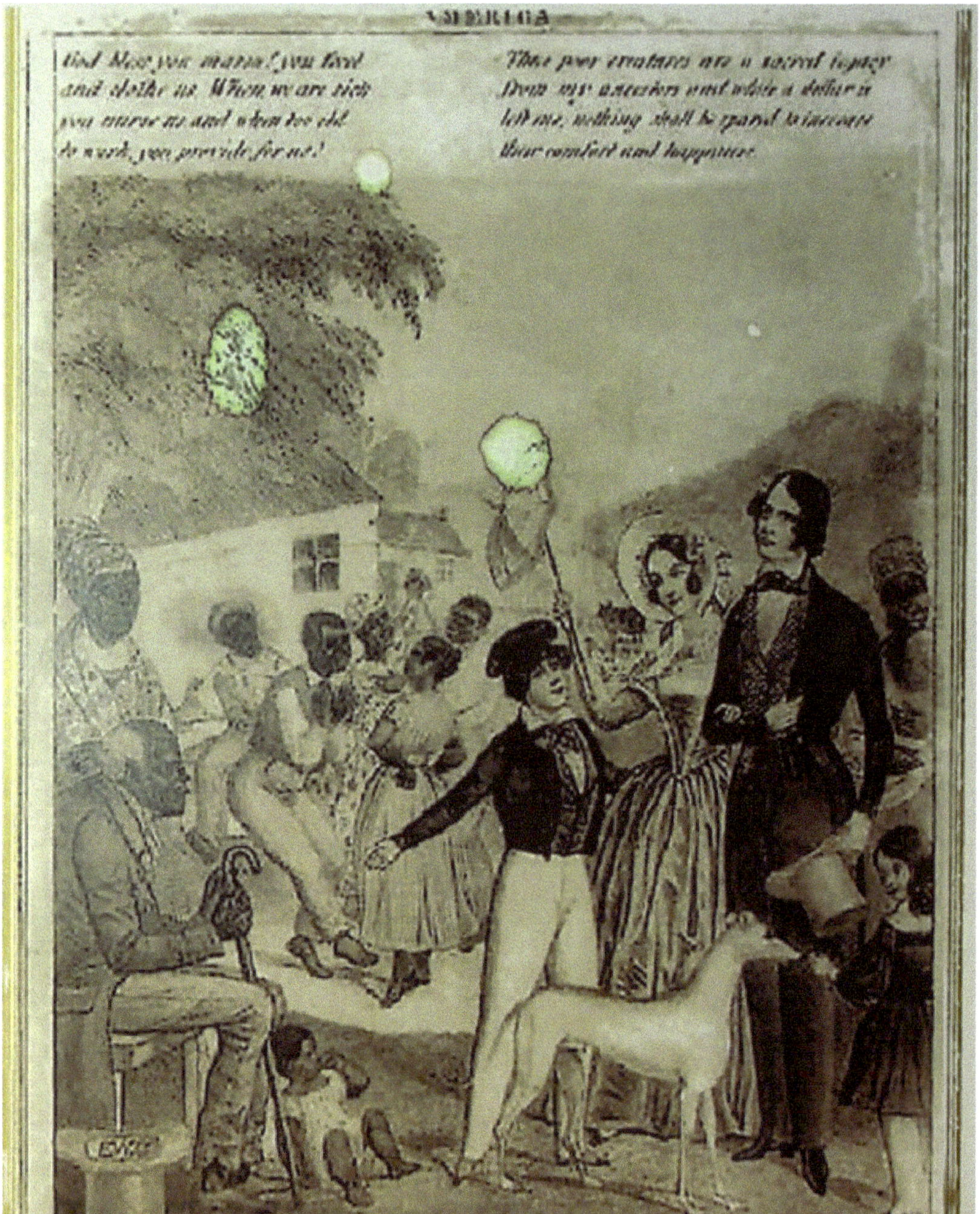

Figure 1.--Here is an drawing from a pre-Civil War War publication in the South depicting an idealized image of slavery of course from the slave-holders point of view. Unfortunately we do not know in what publication it appeared, but it look likes the 1850s. Images from the north tended to depict the brutality of slavery. Interesting neither depicted the economic importance of the slaves in building America. Source Libery of Congress LC-USZ62-89745

[1839.] Anti-Slavery Almanac. 25

THE NATION ROBBING AN INDIAN CHIEF OF HIS WIFE.

When monarchical Spain governed Florida, many slaves fled thither from republican oppression, and found shelter. One of them, having married an Indian chief, their FREEBORN daughter became the wife of Oceola. She was seized as a slave in 1835, by a person, (who had probably never seen her,) holding the claim of her mother's former master. Oceola attempted to defend his wife, but was overpowered and put in irons, by General Thompson, (our government agent,) who commanded the kidnapping party. What marvel that an Indian Chief, as he looked on his little daughter, and thought of his stolen wife, vowed vengeance on the robbers.

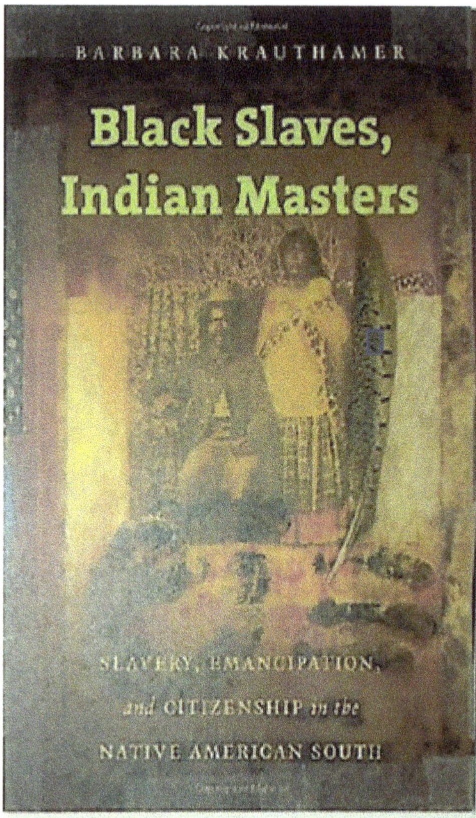

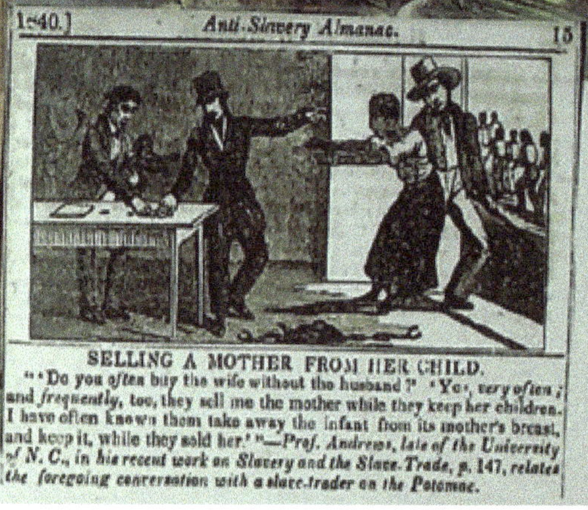
1840.] Anti-Slavery Almanac. 15

SELLING A MOTHER FROM HER CHILD.

"'Do you *often* buy the wife without the husband?' 'Yes, *very often*; and *frequently*, too, they sell me the mother while they keep her children. I have often known them take away the infant from its mother's breast, and keep it, while they sold her.'"—*Prof. Andrews, late of the University of N. C., in his recent work on Slavery and the Slave-Trade, p. 147, relates the foregoing conversation with a slave-trader on the Potomac.*

DOT AND PIN MAPS

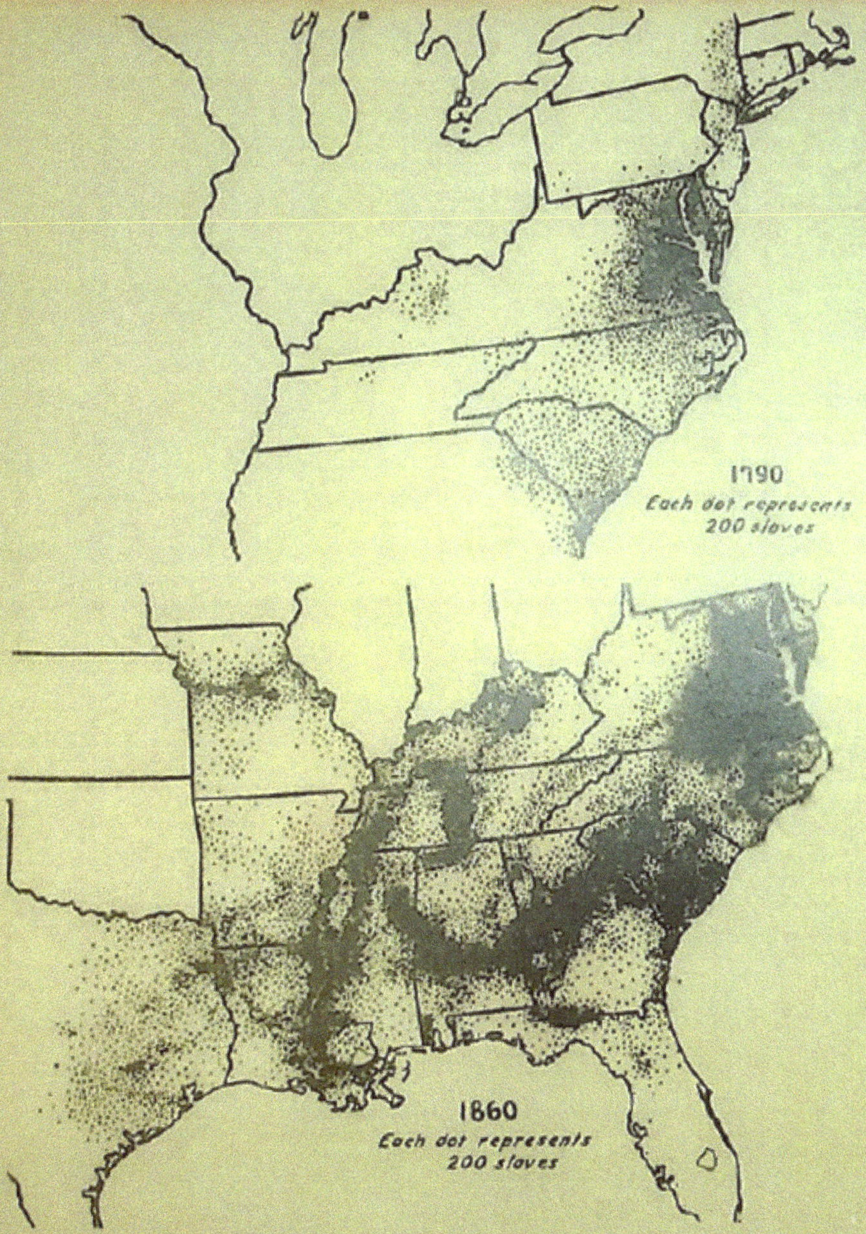

U. S. Department of Agriculture, Bureau of Agricultural Economics. SCALE .8

Number of Slaves in the United States in 1790 and in 1860.

1. These two maps are the first and last of a group of six. Space does not allow all six to be shown here.
2. The use of these two maps in a history lesson would clarify and simplify the slave problem of 1860. This material in tabulated or verbal form would be formidable.
3. Only a section of each map is reproduced here.

5 Native American Communities Who Owned Enslaved Africans
By Barbara-Shae Jackson - April 9, 2014

Cherokee

Cherokee is the largest tribal nation in the United States. They also held more Black slaves than any other Native American community. By 1860, the Cherokee had 4,600 slaves.

Those Black people held captive revolted against the Cherokee in 1842.

Chickasaw

The Chickasaw also held enslaved Africans of their own, and the system they established closely approximated that of white slaveholders on cotton plantations.

Five Things to Know About the Descendants of Cherokee's Black Slaves

Yes, The Cherokee had slaves, and no, their descendants are not happy. They're so unhappy, in fact That they have sued the Cherokee nation that enslaved and freed their ancestors, only to kick them out a century later. On Saturday they'll be gathering in Tulsa, Oklahoma, to prepare for next month's court proceedings. What do they want? To be recognized as part of the Cherokee nation again, of course. Confused? You're not alone.

The group, known as the Freedmen, have been fighting the Cherokee government for citizenship since it was revoked in the early 1980s on the basis that they lacked proof of native blood. Today around 3,000 reservation residents claim lineage from blacks once enslaved by the Cherokee and the rights they were entitled to.

ABOUT
Colonel Vaughan Witten

Colonel Vaughan Witten was born on 18 February 1935 in a small coal mining town of Anawalt, McDowell County, West Virginia to Alphonso Witten of Anawalt and Arlene Walker Witten of Martinsville, Virginia. Wonderful parents, his dad a coal miner for about 40 years and a Baptist Minister for 30 years, and his mom - an Angel from heaven was beyond wonderful. She could do anything, make "bricks without straw", Love everyone, and seemed to never be stressed, insecure or uncertain. A true gift from God for mankind. Colonel's father died in 1991, and his mom in 2000. He has 5 siblings, Audrey, Sandra, Janita, James, and Emma. All doing well, except Audrey died in 2016.

Dr. Witten (Psychologist PhD, of North Carolina State University-Raleigh) was educated in a small one room schoolhouse in Ward, W. VA near the coal mine, with one great teacher Mrs. Louise Henderson -who was the 2nd angel in his life, teaching six different grades in the four corners and center of the room near the pot belly stove for heat in the winter. He eventually graduated early from high school (Booker T Washington High) in his 15th year. After working at cutting grass, bus boy, golf caddy, dish washer, newspaper boy, shoeshine boy, and bowling pin setter for two years until he was eligible for working in the coal mines or entry into the military, he finally joined the U.S. Air Force with the permission of his parents at the age of 17. He eventually served 27 years before retiring in 1979, having risen to the highest enlisted rank of Command Chief Master Sergeant, earned the Bronze Star Medal in his war time Service in Vietnam of 3 tours and stationed in other countries of Greece, England, Greenland, Iceland, Philippines, Japan, Azores Islands, Thailand, Germany and New Foundland.

On the academic side, between duty overseas, Dr. Witten earned a Bachelor's degree in Sociology, a Master's degree in Psychology; and a doctorate PhD in Psychology from N.C. State University in 1989- after he retired from the Air Force. He is currently enjoying life with the flora and fauna of nature, riding his bike and writing books about what he has gleaned from life in 82 years in this world. He is still mourning the loss of his loving wife Mildred who passed in2007, after a wonderful marriage of 50 years.

Dr. Witten's 500-page autobiography "THE JOURNEY": Appalachia to Paradise to Purgatory was completed, published and distributed world-wide by mail, hand and internet on his website in2013. The primary countries are the United States, China, Japan, South Korea, Spain, Greece, India, England, Australia, Italy, Germany, Egypt, Brazil, Philippines, France, Malaysia, Laos, United Kingdom, Chile, Argentina, Portugal, Canada, Mexico and Romania so far, including 38 states in the U.S. It's Free by clicking on www. Colonel Vaughan Witten, com. Over 800 reads, reviews or downloads so far. It's about West Virginia and his world travels- adventures for posterity.

WILD, WONDERFUL, WEST VIRGINIA

This journey from the friendly, exciting mountains and valleys of pristine West Virginia in the 1940s and 1950s to the military life and eye-opening world view of the U.S. Air Force was exceedingly joyful. This West Virginia in which 30 counties in 1863 split off from Virginia over the issue of slavery which it opposed and became a state in its own right; originally proposed to be named Kanawha, then Western Virginia and ultimately, West Virginia. This West Virginia with its hardy, honest, industrious people that was Jim Crow on the surface, but tolerant and integrated in its heart, was the fertile soul the Witten family and many other Blacks labored, loved and lived in pursuit of happiness and attainable success and fortune. Looking back on my youth in Kanawha County, roaming the hills and valleys barefoot, swimming in the mighty Kanawha River and exploring the coal field activities; I realize that I was truly blessed to be in a virtual paradise of physical environment and familial love. Though technically poor by economic standards, and purportedly racially oppressed, I didn't realize or perceive either of those conditions and enjoyed a healthy, free, open, exciting and wonderful childhood attributed mostly to my Mom and Dad because I didn't know I was supposed to be second class and because I didn't know I was not more poor than the typical West Virginian, I escaped the social-psychological scars and baggage that usually accompanies such a background. From such an environment as this, I left home at age 17 with my high school diploma and unlimited confidence in myself to succeed and make my mark on the world. This was the second phase of my journey that began with my enlistment in the U.S. Air Force during the Korean War in 1952.

The continuation of 27 years of globetrotting Air Force duty and the 50 years of marriage to Mildred was paradise, unrealized until it was over. My retirement from the Air Force in 1979 and the loss of my wife in 2007 spanned the years of essential purgatory where I was introduced to the real pain and suffering of life in America and the epiphany of the gradual decline of morals, values, respect and helplessness in observing our slide on the slippery slope of gradual cultural decline. This slide was mitigated by the love and support of my wife Mildred, my sons Scott and Brian and my many friends at Shaw University and different venues in my daily life, including Uncle Elmer and his wife Aunt Bernice, Aunt Gracie, my siblings James, Audrey, Sandra, Janita, Emma and my wonderful parents Arlene and Alphonso Witten until their deaths in 2000 and 1991 respectively. I realize at this writing in my 73rd year, that I have been specially blessed by God and appreciate Him even more because I have not been a faithful churchgoer, but I have been a faithful believer in Jesus and the afterlife of heaven. I feel fortunate for being bom and raised in the United States of America and hope and pray that it can survive the terrorist attacks and immorality of its people in the future.

PSYCHOLOGY OFFICE SHAW UNIVERSITY

Boeing B-52 Stratofortress

posted by Jiri Wagner

C-133 Cargomaster

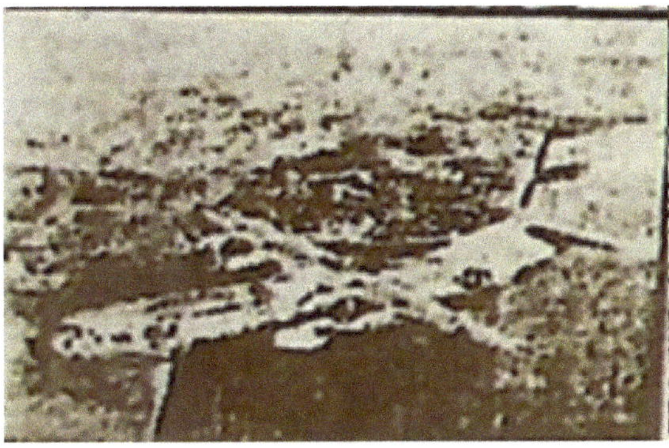

Douglas C-124C *Globemaster* (Courtesy US Air Force Museum)

North Carolina State University

On the recommendation of the Faculty and by virtue of the authority vested in them, the Trustees of the University have conferred on

Colonel Vaughan Witten

the degree of

Doctor of Philosophy

In testimony whereof, the seal of the University and the signatures of its officers are hereunto affixed this ninth day of August, nineteen eighty-nine.

Chairman of the Board of Governors

President of the University of North Carolina

Chairman of the Board of Trustees

Chancellor

Dean, Graduate School

CHINA
INDIA
BANGLADESH
MYANMAR
(BURMA)
THAILAND
CAMBODIA
VIETNAM
MALAYSIA
MALAYA
INDONESIA
SINGAPORE
MEKONG
SOUTH CHINA
SEA
ANDAMAN
100°
110°
5,000 m.
2,000 m.
1,000 m.
500 m.
200 m.
100 m.
Sea
Level Below
North Tropic Line
(Tropic of Cancer)
Bangkok
Hanoi
INDOCHINESE
AND MALAYAN
PENINSULAS

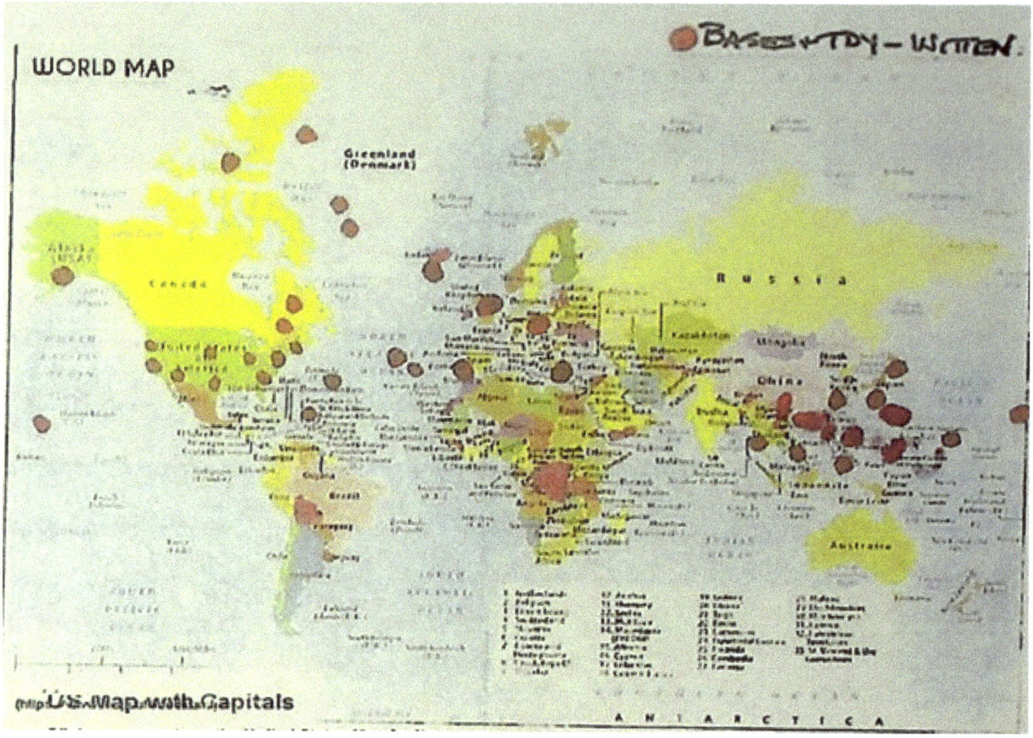
WORLD MAP
BASES + TDY – WITTEN.
Greenland (Denmark)
Russia
Canada
China
Australia
US Map with Capitals
ANTARCTICA

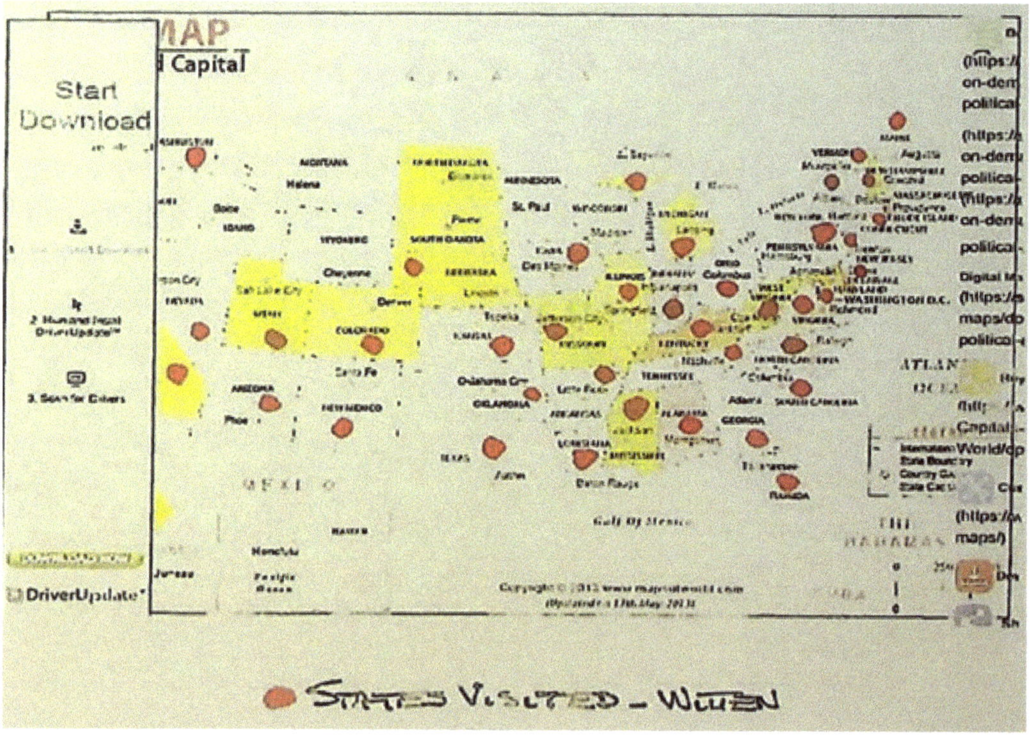
MAP
Capital
Start Download
DriverUpdate
Gulf Of Mexico
STATES VISITED – WITTEN

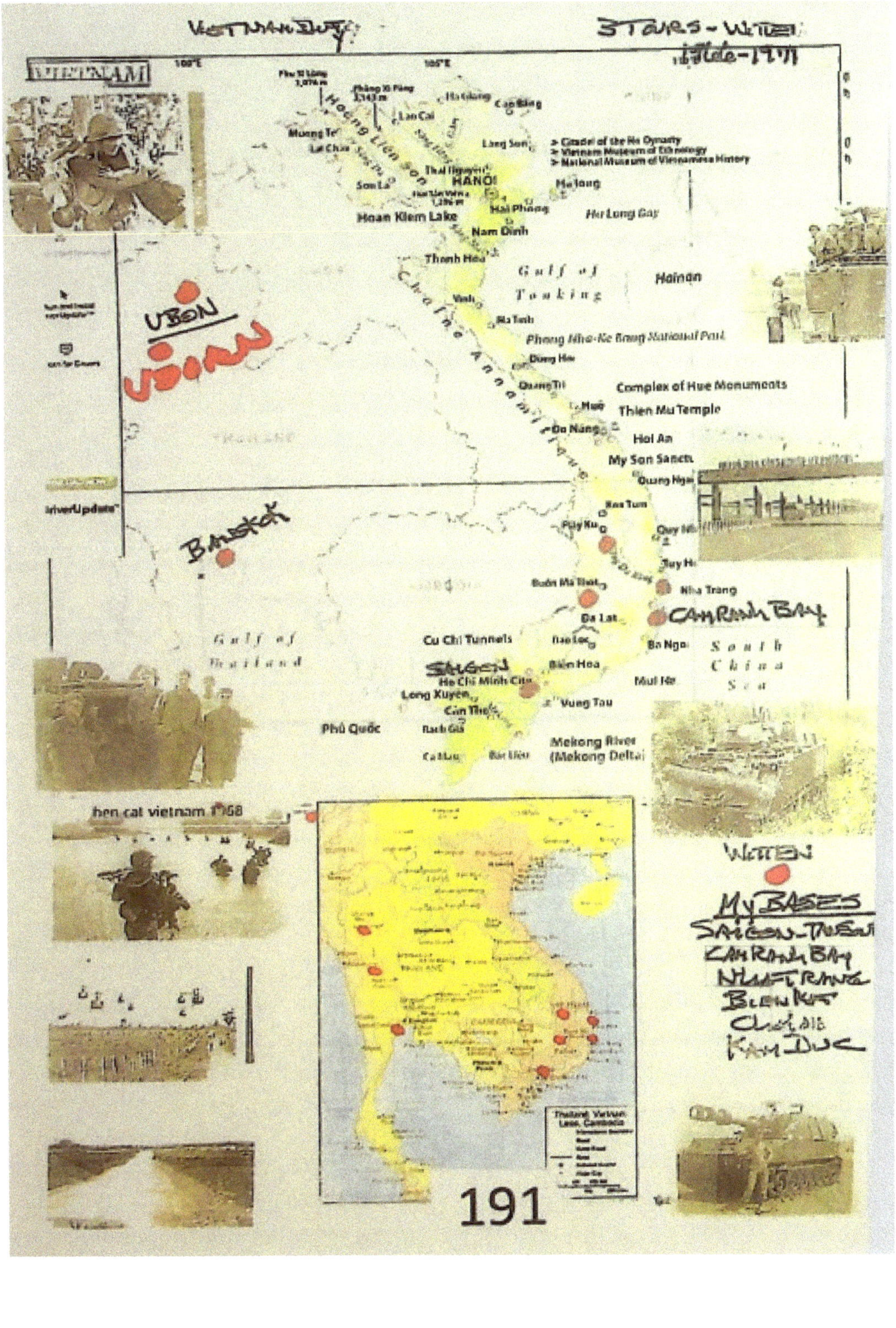
3 TOURS - WITTEN
VIETNAM
Lao Cai
Lang Son
Thai Nguyen
HANOI
Son La
Hai Phong
Ha Long Bay
Hoan Kiem Lake
Nam Dinh
Thanh Hoa
Gulf of Tonking
Hainan
UBON
Phong Nha-Ke Bang National Park
Quang Tri
Complex of Hue Monuments
Hue
Thien Mu Temple
Da Nang
Hoi An
My Son Sanct.
Kon Tum
BANGKOK
Nha Trang
Buon Ma Thuot
Da Lat
CAM RANH BAY
Gulf of Thailand
Cu Chi Tunnels
SAIGON
Bien Hoa
Ho Chi Minh City
Long Xuyen
Can Tho
Vung Tau
Mui Ne
South China Sea
Phú Quốc
Mekong River
(Mekong Delta)
ben cat vietnam 1968
WITTEN
MY BASES
CAM RANH BAY
191

CHAPTER ELEVEN

Summary and Conclusion about Slave Ownership by Free Blacks and American Indians

That African American Slaves were owned by Freed Blacks and many Native American (Indians), is an accepted fact of our history is an uncomfortable truth, yet REAL, and must be acknowledged and processed from a mental health perspective. Many of us Blacks prefer to deny, distort, or rationalize reality that we don't like or consider too painful, at the conscious and the unconscious level. Anthony Johnson as a Freed Black slave owner and even worse, responsible for starting the practice of LIFE long servitude of African Blacks through his court case recovery of his slave John Casor (Castor) in 1655 is almost unbelievable, for we generally think slavery was only practiced by the WHITE man, On top of that, we must deal with the fact that American Indians also owned Black and other Indian slaves especially the Cherokees, Creeks, Chickasaws, Choctaws and Seminoles; about 10,000 in all with the Cherokees owning 4600 of the total, Burton, Art. (1996) Cherokee Slave Revolt 1842, Free Republic News.

In regard to the legacy and impact of Slavery on the current Black population, the historical evidence and current behavior of this population indicates that the effect has been very significantly negative. However not strong or pervasive enough to justify or support the fear, hate, disrespect, unlawful and rebellious behavior of much of the Black race in America. But the sentiments and activities of the "silent majority" of lawful, patriotic, independent thinking and constructive Blacks; have been hijacked by a significant minority of lawless, self-hating, destructive Blacks along with race baiting, race hustling activist and Idiot politicians has created a climate in which the minority "tail is wagging the majority dog" so to speak, and thusly painting ALL Blacks with the SAME unruly, hostile, destructive brush. The sad REALITY now is that the approximately 70% mentioned earlier have LEARNED to be HELPLESS, Colonel V Witten, (2017) which has devolved into a situation where they REJECT the opportunities to advance or improve their situation by ESCAPING TO FREEDOM and the independence that comes with it; BUT rather to ESCAPE FROM FREEDOM and remain in a more "familiar and comfortable cocoon" of dependency of the government welfare check, EBT card and all of the other "candy" and freebies that come at the PRICE of their

INDEPENENCE and SELF reliance, Colonel V. Witten,(2017). AS for the future, it does appear to be bleak with 73% of Black babies born OUT of wedlock, and the following Bad news:

-Total U.S. Welfare 68 million
SNAP-FOOD STAMP 42 million
White welfare 18% /II million
Black welfare 40% /27 million
Hispanic welfare 21% / 12 million

-College Graduation Rate
White 86% Hispanic 73% Black 69 %

-High School Graduation Rate
Total U.S. 83%
Asian/Pacific 90%
White 88%
Black 75%
Hispanic 78%
Indian/Alaskan 72%

U.S. Department of Commerce and National Center for Education statistics, (2014-2015).

> Median Income U.S. 2013
White $ 67,000
Asian $68,000
Hispanic $40,000
Black $39,000: Pew Research (2013)

> Unemployment 2016
Total U.S. 4.4%
White 4.3%, Hispanic 5.9%, Black 8.8%
Brietbart.com, (2016).

Black Voting Profile, 90% Democrat PRESIDENT

Al Gore 2000, Dem 92%- Repub. 8% John Kerry 2004, 88% -Repub. 12% Barak Obama 2008, 96%-Repub.4% H. Clinton 2016, 88%-Repub. 12% Black Voter Turnout-Election, (2016) Theybf. (2016). Blacks vote Democrat like robots, though they get basically nothing but unfulfilled promises- YET they persist in FOLLY.

John Horse

John Horse, also known as Juan Caballo, John Cowaya and Gopher John, was born in 1812 in Florida of a Black mother and an Indian father. He was described as six feet tall, muscular, and \s leader of the Black Seminoles, John Horse struggled for almost half a century to obtain land and a permanent home for his people. He was a warrior against the United States during the Second Seminole War. To gain his freedom, he served the U.S. Army as a guide and interpreter In the Indian Territory, he founded the village of Wewoka for his followers and made several trips to Washington, D.C., to lobby government officials on their behalf. John Horse, as second in-command to the Seminole Indian Chief Coacoochee (Wild Cat), led more than one hundred Black Seminoles from Indian Territory to Mexico. From 1850 to 1870 he was head of the Black Seminole community in Nacimiento, Coahuila, Mexico, and took some of them back to Texas for service as scouts with the U.S. Army. The men were promised land after their service as scouts. but this promise never materialized. John Horse, old and recovering from wounds following an assassination attempt, returned to his home in Nacimiento. He died in Mexico City in 1882 while on a mission to settle a dispute over their land.

Wild Cat, also known as *Coacoochee* or *Cowacoochee* (From Creek *Kowakkuce* "bobcat, wildcat"^ (c.1807/1810-1857) was a leading Seminole chieftain during the later stages of the Second Seminole War as well as the nephew of Micanopy.

Wild Cat's exact place year and place of birth is not agreed upon. Many local scholars believe he was born in 1807 on an island in big Lake Tohopekaliga, south of Orlando. some scholars say Wild Cat was born to King Philip (or Ee-mat-la) in Yulaka, a Seminole village along the St. Johns River in northern Florida around 1810. Still others suggest that he was born near present-day Apopka, Florida J5J Wild Cat may have had a twin sister who died at birth and, having been born a twin, he was regarded by the tribe as being particularly gifted. As tensions mounted between Seminoles and local settlers following the purchase of Florida by the United States in 1821, Seminole tribes encouraged the escape of slaves in neighboring Georgia in reaction to encroaching settlers who began settling on the Florida coast previously occupied by Seminoles.

Wild Cat (Seminole)

REFERENCES

Anti - Slavery Society, (2011) Human Trafficking.
Bandler, A. (2016) Black Crime and Murder. Banks, T.L.
(2009) Eliz. Keys Freedom suit.
BBC. (2011), The Abolition Season.
Black Demographics, com (2017) Facts about the African American population.
Britannica Encyclopedia, (2011).
Burton, A. T. (1996) Cherokee Slave Revolt of!842. Free Republic.
CBS. Philly Report, (2014). Black Males Arrested before their 23rd birthday. CBS
Code of Hammurabi circa (1620) BC-2017.
Dalco, Frederick. (1823) South Carolina Clergyman, Practical Considerations Founded on Scriptures, Richmond Enquirer.
Deborrah (Cooper), (2010), Emotionally Abusive Black Man-Surviving Dating.com.
Deconde, A. (1963) A History of American Foreign Policy.
Publisher-Scribner (1971).
Digital History.oh.edu.(2013) Slave impact.
Foner, Philip . (1980) "History of Black Americans: From Africa to the emergence of the cotton kingdom". Oxford Univ. Press.
Gardner, Howard. (2017). Harvard School of Education. Ml Intelligence, Oasis.org
Gift, S.l. (2008) Maroon Teachers: Teaching the Trans Atlantic trade in Enslaved Africans. Randle Publishers.
Goldman, Lynn. (1998) GWU Pub. Health.
Grooms, Robert M. (1998). "Dixie's Censored Secret: Black Slave Owners.
Grooms, R. M. (2014) Jamestown 1619.
Harris, V.A. (1999) Demography Roman Slav
Heinegg, Paul, (2010) Freed African American slaves in Va., N.C., S.C., Md and De. (http:// freeafricanamericans.com./)

Holloway, Joseph E. (2015) The Slave Rebellion, Amazon.com.
Ironbark Resources, (2013) White Slaves, Black Slave Traders, and the hidden history of slavery, American Heritage.
Jackson, B. (2014) Atlanta Black Star, Native American Communities of Slave Owners.
Johnson, C., McCune, G. (2011).
Klein, H.S. (2007) The Middle Slave passage.
Klein, H. & Vinson, B. (2007) African Slavery .in Latin America and the Caribbean 2nd ed.
Koger, Larry. (1985) Black Slave Owners, Free Black Slave Masters in South Carolina.
Law Library of Congress (2017)
Maddison, A., (2008), The Portuguese in Brazil. The World Economy.org.
Martis, K. C. (1994) Historical Atlas of CSA.
Merton, R. K. (1938). Social Structure arid Anomie. American Sociological Review.
Morrison, L. (1823) Religious Defense of American Slavery before 1830
Olafson,S. (2011) Slave descendants expeld,
Pagden, Anthony. (1998), Human Slavery
Painter, Nell Irvin (2006) Creating Black American History and it's meaning.
PBS.org. (2013). Unhealthy Food-Black diet.
Plomin, Kennedy. & Craig (2005) Riordan, Patrick: "Finding freedom in Florida: Native peoples, African Americans, and Colonists 1670 - 1816. Florida Historical Quarterly, (1996).
Russell, John H. (1916) Free Negro-Virginia
Sentencing Project (2017) Blacks expected to go to prison in their lifetime Wash. D.C.
Sowell, T. (2012) Race, IQ, and Black Crime. Swartz, A. (2009) Mental Health.com.
VogelerJ. (1985) Tree Black Slave Owners.
Wil1iams, H.A.(2017)How Slavery affected African American Families.
Univ. N. C. Witten, Colonel Vaughan, (2017) Escape from Freedom: The Fallacy of Victimism, and Resulting Self Defeating Behavior and Avoidance of Responsibility. (SELF)
Witten, Colonel Vaughan, (2017) Learned Helplessness: The Poison Pill Tbre_aX to Black America. (SELF)
Wood, William. (1970) The illegal beginning of American Slavery. ABA Journal, Acc.2011.